The Man from Snowy River and Other Verses

Andrew Barton `Banjo' Paterson

Table of Contents

Table of Contents

The Man from Snowy River and Other

Andrew Barton `Banjo' Paterson

Preface

It is not so easy to write ballads descriptive of the bushland of Australia as on light consideration would appear. Reasonably good verse on the subject has been supplied in sufficient quantity. But the maker of folksongs for our newborn nation requires a somewhat rare combination of gifts and experiences. Dowered with the poet's heart, he must yet have passed his `wander–jaehre' amid the stern solitude of the Austral waste — must have ridden the race in the back–block township, guided the reckless stock–horse adown the mountain spur, and followed the night–long moving, spectral–seeming herd `in the droving days'. Amid such scarce congenial surroundings comes oft that finer sense which renders visible bright gleams of humour, pathos, and romance, which, like undiscovered gold, await the fortunate adventurer. That the author has touched this treasure–trove, not less delicately than distinctly, no true Australian will deny. In my opinion this collection comprises the best bush ballads written since the death of Lindsay Gordon.

Rolf Boldrewood

A number of these verses are now published for the first time, most of the others were written for and appeared in "The Bulletin" (Sydney, N.S.W.), and are therefore already widely known to readers in Australasia.

A. B. Paterson

Prelude

I have gathered these stories afar,
 In the wind and the rain,
In the land where the cattle camps are,
 On the edge of the plain.
On the overland routes of the west,
 When the watches were long,
I have fashioned in earnest and jest
 These fragments of song.

They are just the rude stories one hears

In sadness and mirth,
The records of wandering years,
And scant is their worth
Though their merits indeed are but slight,
I shall not repine,
If they give you one moment's delight,
Old comrades of mine.

The Man from Snowy River

There was movement at the station, for the word had passed around
That the colt from old Regret had got away,
And had joined the wild bush horses — he was worth a thousand pound,
So all the cracks had gathered to the fray.
All the tried and noted riders from the stations near and far
Had mustered at the homestead overnight,
For the bushmen love hard riding where the wild bush horses are,
And the stock–horse snuffs the battle with delight.

There was Harrison, who made his pile when Pardon won the cup,
The old man with his hair as white as snow;

But few could ride beside him when his blood was fairly up —
He would go wherever horse and man could go.
And Clancy of the Overflow came down to lend a hand,
No better horseman ever held the reins;
For never horse could throw him while the saddle–girths would stand,
He learnt to ride while droving on the plains.

And one was there, a stripling on a small and weedy beast,
He was something like a racehorse undersized,
With a touch of Timor pony — three parts thoroughbred at least —
And such as are by mountain horsemen prized.
He was hard and tough and wiry — just the sort that won't say die —
There was courage in his quick impatient tread;
And he bore the badge of gameness in his bright and fiery eye,
And the proud and lofty carriage of his head.

But still so slight and weedy, one would doubt his power to stay,
And the old man said, `That horse will never do
For a long and tiring gallop — lad, you'd better stop away,
Those hills are far too rough for such as you.'
So he waited sad and wistful — only Clancy stood his friend —
`I think we ought to let him come,' he said;
`I warrant he'll be with us when he's wanted at the end,
For both his horse and he are mountain bred.

`He hails from Snowy River, up by Kosciusko's side,
Where the hills are twice as steep and twice as rough,
Where a horse's hoofs strike firelight from the flint stones every stride,
The man that holds his own is good enough.
And the Snowy River riders on the mountains make their home,
Where the river runs those giant hills between;
I have seen full many horsemen since I first commenced to roam,
But nowhere yet such horsemen have I seen.'

So he went — they found the horses by the big mimosa clump —
They raced away towards the mountain's brow,

And the old man gave his orders, `Boys, go at them from the jump,
No use to try for fancy riding now.
And, Clancy, you must wheel them, try and wheel them to the right.
Ride boldly, lad, and never fear the spills,
For never yet was rider that could keep the mob in sight,
If once they gain the shelter of those hills.'

So Clancy rode to wheel them — he was racing on the wing
Where the best and boldest riders take their place,
And he raced his stock–horse past them, and he made the ranges ring
With the stockwhip, as he met them face to face.
Then they halted for a moment, while he swung the dreaded lash,
But they saw their well–loved mountain full in view,
And they charged beneath the stockwhip with a sharp and sudden dash,
And off into the mountain scrub they flew.

Then fast the horsemen followed, where the gorges deep and black
Resounded to the thunder of their tread,
And the stockwhips woke the echoes, and they fiercely answered back
From cliffs and crags that beetled overhead.
And upward, ever upward, the wild horses held their way,
Where mountain ash and kurrajong grew wide;
And the old man muttered fiercely, `We may bid the mob good day,
NO man can hold them down the other side.'

When they reached the mountain's summit, even Clancy took a pull,
It well might make the boldest hold their breath,
The wild hop scrub grew thickly, and the hidden ground was full
Of wombat holes, and any slip was death.
But the man from Snowy River let the pony have his head,
And he swung his stockwhip round and gave a cheer,
And he raced him down the mountain like a torrent down its bed,
While the others stood and watched in very fear.

He sent the flint stones flying, but the pony kept his feet,
He cleared the fallen timber in his stride,

And the man from Snowy River never shifted in his seat —
It was grand to see that mountain horseman ride.
Through the stringy barks and saplings, on the rough and broken ground,
Down the hillside at a racing pace he went;
And he never drew the bridle till he landed safe and sound,
At the bottom of that terrible descent.

He was right among the horses as they climbed the further hill,
And the watchers on the mountain standing mute,
Saw him ply the stockwhip fiercely, he was right among them still,
As he raced across the clearing in pursuit.
Then they lost him for a moment, where two mountain gullies met
In the ranges, but a final glimpse reveals
On a dim and distant hillside the wild horses racing yet,
With the man from Snowy River at their heels.

And he ran them single–handed till their sides were white with foam.
He followed like a bloodhound on their track,
Till they halted cowed and beaten, then he turned their heads for home,
And alone and unassisted brought them back.
But his hardy mountain pony he could scarcely raise a trot,
He was blood from hip to shoulder from the spur;
But his pluck was still undaunted, and his courage fiery hot,
For never yet was mountain horse a cur.

And down by Kosciusko, where the pine–clad ridges raise
Their torn and rugged battlements on high,
Where the air is clear as crystal, and the white stars fairly blaze
At midnight in the cold and frosty sky,
And where around the Overflow the reedbeds sweep and sway
To the breezes, and the rolling plains are wide,
The man from Snowy River is a household word to–day,
And the stockmen tell the story of his ride.

Old Pardon, the Son of Reprieve

You never heard tell of the story?
 Well, now, I can hardly believe!
Never heard of the honour and glory
 Of Pardon, the son of Reprieve?
But maybe you're only a Johnnie
 And don't know a horse from a hoe?
Well, well, don't get angry, my sonny,
 But, really, a young un should know.

They bred him out back on the `Never',
 His mother was Mameluke breed.
To the front — and then stay there — was ever
 The root of the Mameluke creed.
He seemed to inherit their wiry
 Strong frames — and their pluck to receive —
As hard as a flint and as fiery
 Was Pardon, the son of Reprieve.

We ran him at many a meeting
 At crossing and gully and town,
And nothing could give him a beating —
 At least when our money was down.
For weight wouldn't stop him, nor distance,
 Nor odds, though the others were fast,
He'd race with a dogged persistence,
 And wear them all down at the last.

At the Turon the Yattendon filly
 Led by lengths at the mile–and–a–half,
And we all began to look silly,
 While HER crowd were starting to laugh;
But the old horse came faster and faster,
 His pluck told its tale, and his strength,
He gained on her, caught her, and passed her,
 And won it, hands–down, by a length.

And then we swooped down on Menindie
 To run for the President's Cup —
Oh! that's a sweet township — a shindy
 To them is board, lodging, and sup.
Eye–openers they are, and their system
 Is never to suffer defeat;
It's `win, tie, or wrangle' — to best 'em
 You must lose 'em, or else it's `dead heat'.

We strolled down the township and found 'em
 At drinking and gaming and play;
If sorrows they had, why they drowned 'em,
 And betting was soon under way.
Their horses were good 'uns and fit 'uns,
 There was plenty of cash in the town;
They backed their own horses like Britons,
 And, Lord! how WE rattled it down!

With gladness we thought of the morrow,
 We counted our wagers with glee,
A simile homely to borrow —
 `There was plenty of milk in our tea.'
You see we were green; and we never
 Had even a thought of foul play,
Though we well might have known that the clever
 Division would `put us away'.

Experience `docet', they tell us,
At least so I've frequently heard,
But, `dosing' or `stuffing', those fellows
Were up to each move on the board:
They got to his stall — it is sinful
To think what such villains would do —
And they gave him a regular skinful
Of barley — green barley — to chew.

He munched it all night, and we found him
Next morning as full as a hog —
The girths wouldn't nearly meet round him;
He looked like an overfed frog.
We saw we were done like a dinner —
The odds were a thousand to one
Against Pardon turning up winner,
'Twas cruel to ask him to run.

We got to the course with our troubles,
A crestfallen couple were we;
And we heard the `books' calling the doubles —
A roar like the surf of the sea;
And over the tumult and louder
Rang `Any price Pardon, I lay!'
Says Jimmy, `The children of Judah
Are out on the warpath to–day.'

Three miles in three heats: — Ah, my sonny,
The horses in those days were stout,
They had to run well to win money;
I don't see such horses about.
Your six–furlong vermin that scamper
Half–a–mile with their feather–weight up;
They wouldn't earn much of their damper
In a race like the President's Cup.

The first heat was soon set a–going;
The Dancer went off to the front;
The Don on his quarters was showing,
With Pardon right out of the hunt.
He rolled and he weltered and wallowed —
You'd kick your hat faster, I'll bet;
They finished all bunched, and he followed
All lathered and dripping with sweat.

But troubles came thicker upon us,
For while we were rubbing him dry
The stewards came over to warn us:
`We hear you are running a bye!
If Pardon don't spiel like tarnation
And win the next heat — if he can —
He'll earn a disqualification;
Just think over THAT, now, my man!'

Our money all gone and our credit,
Our horse couldn't gallop a yard;
And then people thought that WE did it!
It really was terribly hard.
We were objects of mirth and derision
To folk in the lawn and the stand,
And the yells of the clever division
Of `Any price Pardon!' were grand.

We still had a chance for the money,
Two heats still remained to be run;
If both fell to us — why, my sonny,
The clever division were done.
And Pardon was better, we reckoned,
His sickness was passing away,
So he went to the post for the second
And principal heat of the day.

They're off and away with a rattle,
Like dogs from the leashes let slip,
And right at the back of the battle
He followed them under the whip.
They gained ten good lengths on him quickly
He dropped right away from the pack;
I tell you it made me feel sickly
To see the blue jacket fall back.

Our very last hope had departed —
We thought the old fellow was done,
When all of a sudden he started
To go like a shot from a gun.
His chances seemed slight to embolden
Our hearts; but, with teeth firmly set,
We thought, `Now or never! The old 'un
May reckon with some of 'em yet.'

Then loud rose the war–cry for Pardon;
He swept like the wind down the dip,
And over the rise by the garden,
The jockey was done with the whip
The field were at sixes and sevens —
The pace at the first had been fast —
And hope seemed to drop from the heavens,
For Pardon was coming at last.

And how he did come! It was splendid;
He gained on them yards every bound,
Stretching out like a greyhound extended,
His girth laid right down on the ground.
A shimmer of silk in the cedars
As into the running they wheeled,
And out flashed the whips on the leaders,
For Pardon had collared the field.

Then right through the ruck he came sailing —
 I knew that the battle was won —
The son of Haphazard was failing,
 The Yattendon filly was done;
He cut down the Don and the Dancer,
 He raced clean away from the mare —
He's in front! Catch him now if you can, sir!
 And up went my hat in the air!

Then loud from the lawn and the garden
 Rose offers of `Ten to one ON!'
`Who'll bet on the field? I back Pardon!'
 No use; all the money was gone.
He came for the third heat light–hearted,
 A–jumping and dancing about;
The others were done ere they started
 Crestfallen, and tired, and worn out.

He won it, and ran it much faster
 Than even the first, I believe
Oh, he was the daddy, the master,
 Was Pardon, the son of Reprieve.
He showed 'em the method to travel —
 The boy sat as still as a stone —
They never could see him for gravel;
 He came in hard–held, and alone.

. . . . .

But he's old — and his eyes are grown hollow;
 Like me, with my thatch of the snow;
When he dies, then I hope I may follow,
 And go where the racehorses go.
I don't want no harping nor singing —
 Such things with my style don't agree;
Where the hoofs of the horses are ringing

There's music sufficient for me.

And surely the thoroughbred horses
Will rise up again and begin
Fresh races on far–away courses,
And p'raps they might let me slip in.
It would look rather well the race–card on
'Mongst Cherubs and Seraphs and things,
`Angel Harrison's black gelding Pardon,
Blue halo, white body and wings.'

And if they have racing hereafter,
(And who is to say they will not?)
When the cheers and the shouting and laughter
Proclaim that the battle grows hot;
As they come down the racecourse a–steering,
He'll rush to the front, I believe;
And you'll hear the great multitude cheering
For Pardon, the son of Reprieve.

Clancy of the Overflow

I had written him a letter which I had, for want of better
Knowledge, sent to where I met him down the Lachlan, years ago,
He was shearing when I knew him, so I sent the letter to him,
Just `on spec', addressed as follows, `Clancy, of The Overflow'.

And an answer came directed in a writing unexpected,
(And I think the same was written with a thumb–nail dipped in tar)
'Twas his shearing mate who wrote it, and verbatim I will quote it:
`Clancy's gone to Queensland droving, and we don't know where he are.'

. . . . .

In my wild erratic fancy visions come to me of Clancy
Gone a–droving `down the Cooper' where the Western drovers go;
As the stock are slowly stringing, Clancy rides behind them singing,
For the drover's life has pleasures that the townsfolk never know.

And the bush hath friends to meet him, and their kindly voices greet him
In the murmur of the breezes and the river on its bars,
And he sees the vision splendid of the sunlit plains extended,
And at night the wond'rous glory of the everlasting stars.

. . . . .

I am sitting in my dingy little office, where a stingy
Ray of sunlight struggles feebly down between the houses tall,
And the foetid air and gritty of the dusty, dirty city
Through the open window floating, spreads its foulness over all

And in place of lowing cattle, I can hear the fiendish rattle
Of the tramways and the 'buses making hurry down the street,
And the language uninviting of the gutter children fighting,
Comes fitfully and faintly through the ceaseless tramp of feet.

And the hurrying people daunt me, and their pallid faces haunt me
As they shoulder one another in their rush and nervous haste,
With their eager eyes and greedy, and their stunted forms and weedy,
For townsfolk have no time to grow, they have no time to waste.

And I somehow rather fancy that I'd like to change with Clancy,
Like to take a turn at droving where the seasons come and go,

While he faced the round eternal of the cash–book and the journal —
 But I doubt he'd suit the office, Clancy, of `The Overflow'.

Conroy's Gap

This was the way of it, don't you know —
 Ryan was `wanted' for stealing sheep,
And never a trooper, high or low,
 Could find him — catch a weasel asleep!
Till Trooper Scott, from the Stockman's Ford —
 A bushman, too, as I've heard them tell —
Chanced to find him drunk as a lord
 Round at the Shadow of Death Hotel.

D'you know the place? It's a wayside inn,
 A low grog–shanty — a bushman trap,
Hiding away in its shame and sin
 Under the shelter of Conroy's Gap —
Under the shade of that frowning range,
 The roughest crowd that ever drew breath —
Thieves and rowdies, uncouth and strange,
 Were mustered round at the Shadow of Death.

The trooper knew that his man would slide
 Like a dingo pup, if he saw the chance;
And with half a start on the mountain side
 Ryan would lead him a merry dance.

Drunk as he was when the trooper came,
To him that did not matter a rap —
Drunk or sober, he was the same,
The boldest rider in Conroy's Gap.

`I want you, Ryan,' the trooper said,
`And listen to me, if you dare resist,
So help me heaven, I'll shoot you dead!'
He snapped the steel on his prisoner's wrist,
And Ryan, hearing the handcuffs click,
Recovered his wits as they turned to go,
For fright will sober a man as quick
As all the drugs that the doctors know.

There was a girl in that rough bar
Went by the name of Kate Carew,
Quiet and shy as the bush girls are,
But ready–witted and plucky, too.
She loved this Ryan, or so they say,
And passing by, while her eyes were dim
With tears, she said in a careless way,
`The Swagman's round in the stable, Jim.'

Spoken too low for the trooper's ear,
Why should she care if he heard or not?
Plenty of swagmen far and near,
And yet to Ryan it meant a lot.
That was the name of the grandest horse
In all the district from east to west
In every show ring, on every course
They always counted the Swagman best.

He was a wonder, a raking bay —
One of the grand old Snowdon strain —
One of the sort that could race and stay
With his mighty limbs and his length of rein.

Born and bred on the mountain side,
He could race through scrub like a kangaroo,
The girl herself on his back might ride,
And the Swagman would carry her safely through.

He would travel gaily from daylight's flush
Till after the stars hung out their lamps,
There was never his like in the open bush,
And never his match on the cattle–camps.
For faster horses might well be found
On racing tracks, or a plain's extent,
But few, if any, on broken ground
Could see the way that the Swagman went.

When this girl's father, old Jim Carew,
Was droving out on the Castlereagh
With Conroy's cattle, a wire came through
To say that his wife couldn't live the day.
And he was a hundred miles from home,
As flies the crow, with never a track,
Through plains as pathless as ocean's foam,
He mounted straight on the Swagman's back.

He left the camp by the sundown light,
And the settlers out on the Marthaguy
Awoke and heard, in the dead of night,
A single horseman hurrying by.
He crossed the Bogan at Dandaloo,
And many a mile of the silent plain
That lonely rider behind him threw
Before they settled to sleep again.

He rode all night and he steered his course
By the shining stars with a bushman's skill,
And every time that he pressed his horse
The Swagman answered him gamely still.

He neared his home as the east was bright,
The doctor met him outside the town:
`Carew! How far did you come last night?'
`A hundred miles since the sun went down.'

And his wife got round, and an oath he passed,
So long as he or one of his breed
Could raise a coin, though it took their last
The Swagman never should want a feed.
And Kate Carew, when her father died,
She kept the horse and she kept him well:
The pride of the district far and wide,
He lived in style at the bush hotel.

Such was the Swagman; and Ryan knew
Nothing about could pace the crack;
Little he'd care for the man in blue
If once he got on the Swagman's back.
But how to do it? A word let fall
Gave him the hint as the girl passed by;
Nothing but `Swagman — stable–wall;
`Go to the stable and mind your eye.'

He caught her meaning, and quickly turned
To the trooper: `Reckon you'll gain a stripe
By arresting me, and it's easily earned;
Let's go to the stable and get my pipe,
The Swagman has it.' So off they went,
And soon as ever they turned their backs
The girl slipped down, on some errand bent
Behind the stable, and seized an axe.

The trooper stood at the stable door
While Ryan went in quite cool and slow,
And then (the trick had been played before)
The girl outside gave the wall a blow.

Three slabs fell out of the stable wall —
'Twas done 'fore ever the trooper knew —
And Ryan, as soon as he saw them fall,
Mounted the Swagman and rushed him through.

The trooper heard the hoof–beats ring
In the stable yard, and he slammed the gate,
But the Swagman rose with a mighty spring
At the fence, and the trooper fired too late,
As they raced away and his shots flew wide
And Ryan no longer need care a rap,
For never a horse that was lapped in hide
Could catch the Swagman in Conroy's Gap.

And that's the story. You want to know
If Ryan came back to his Kate Carew;
Of course he should have, as stories go,
But the worst of it is, this story's true:
And in real life it's a certain rule,
Whatever poets and authors say
Of high–toned robbers and all their school,
These horsethief fellows aren't built that way.

Come back! Don't hope it — the slinking hound,
He sloped across to the Queensland side,
And sold the Swagman for fifty pound,
And stole the money, and more beside.
And took to drink, and by some good chance
Was killed — thrown out of a stolen trap.
And that was the end of this small romance,
The end of the story of Conroy's Gap.

Our New Horse

The boys had come back from the races
 All silent and down on their luck;
They'd backed 'em, straight out and for places,
 But never a winner they struck.
They lost their good money on Slogan,
 And fell, most uncommonly flat,
When Partner, the pride of the Bogan,
 Was beaten by Aristocrat.

And one said, `I move that instanter
 We sell out our horses and quit,
The brutes ought to win in a canter,
 Such trials they do when they're fit.
The last one they ran was a snorter —
 A gallop to gladden one's heart —
Two–twelve for a mile and a quarter,
 And finished as straight as a dart.

`And then when I think that they're ready
 To win me a nice little swag,
They are licked like the veriest neddy —
 They're licked from the fall of the flag.
The mare held her own to the stable,
 She died out to nothing at that,
And Partner he never seemed able
 To pace it with Aristocrat.

`And times have been bad, and the seasons
 Don't promise to be of the best;

In short, boys, there's plenty of reasons
 For giving the racing a rest.
The mare can be kept on the station —
 Her breeding is good as can be —
But Partner, his next destination
 Is rather a trouble to me.

`We can't sell him here, for they know him
 As well as the clerk of the course;
He's raced and won races till, blow him,
 He's done as a handicap horse.
A jady, uncertain performer,
 They weight him right out of the hunt,
And clap it on warmer and warmer
 Whenever he gets near the front.

`It's no use to paint him or dot him
 Or put any `fake' on his brand,
For bushmen are smart, and they'd spot him
 In any sale–yard in the land.
The folk about here could all tell him,
 Could swear to each separate hair;
Let us send him to Sydney and sell him,
 There's plenty of Jugginses there.

`We'll call him a maiden, and treat 'em
 To trials will open their eyes,
We'll run their best horses and beat 'em,
 And then won't they think him a prize.
I pity the fellow that buys him,
 He'll find in a very short space,
No matter how highly he tries him,
 The beggar won't RACE in a race.'

. . . . .

Next week, under `Seller and Buyer',
 Appeared in the DAILY GAZETTE:
`A racehorse for sale, and a flyer;
 Has never been started as yet;
A trial will show what his pace is;
 The buyer can get him in light,
And win all the handicap races.
 Apply here before Wednesday night.'

He sold for a hundred and thirty,
 Because of a gallop he had
One morning with Bluefish and Bertie,
 And donkey-licked both of 'em bad.
And when the old horse had departed,
 The life on the station grew tame;
The race-track was dull and deserted,
 The boys had gone back on the game.

. . . . .

The winter rolled by, and the station
 Was green with the garland of spring
A spirit of glad exultation
 Awoke in each animate thing.
And all the old love, the old longing,
 Broke out in the breasts of the boys,
The visions of racing came thronging
 With all its delirious joys.

The rushing of floods in their courses,
 The rattle of rain on the roofs
Recalled the fierce rush of the horses,
 The thunder of galloping hoofs.
And soon one broke out: `I can suffer
 No longer the life of a slug,
The man that don't race is a duffer,

Let's have one more run for the mug.

`Why, EVERYTHING races, no matter
Whatever its method may be:
The waterfowl hold a regatta;
The 'possums run heats up a tree;
The emus are constantly sprinting
A handicap out on the plain;
It seems like all nature was hinting,
'Tis time to be at it again.

`The cockatoo parrots are talking
Of races to far away lands;
The native companions are walking
A go–as–you–please on the sands;
The little foals gallop for pastime;
The wallabies race down the gap;
Let's try it once more for the last time,
Bring out the old jacket and cap.

`And now for a horse; we might try one
Of those that are bred on the place,
But I think it better to buy one,
A horse that has proved he can race.
Let us send down to Sydney to Skinner,
A thorough good judge who can ride,
And ask him to buy us a spinner
To clean out the whole countryside.'

They wrote him a letter as follows:
`We want you to buy us a horse;
He must have the speed to catch swallows,
And stamina with it of course.
The price ain't a thing that'll grieve us,
It's getting a bad 'un annoys
The undersigned blokes, and believe us,

We're yours to a cinder, `the boys'.'

He answered: `I've bought you a hummer,
A horse that has never been raced;
I saw him run over the Drummer,
He held him outclassed and outpaced.
His breeding's not known, but they state he
Is born of a thoroughbred strain,
I paid them a hundred and eighty,
And started the horse in the train.'

They met him — alas, that these verses
Aren't up to the subject's demands —
Can't set forth their eloquent curses,
FOR PARTNER WAS BACK ON THEIR HANDS.
They went in to meet him in gladness,
They opened his box with delight —
A silent procession of sadness
They crept to the station at night.

And life has grown dull on the station,
The boys are all silent and slow;
Their work is a daily vexation,
And sport is unknown to them now.
Whenever they think how they stranded,
They squeal just like guinea–pigs squeal;
They bit their own hook, and were landed
With fifty pounds loss on the deal.

An Idyll of Dandaloo

On Western plains, where shade is not,
 'Neath summer skies of cloudless blue,
Where all is dry and all is hot,
 There stands the town of Dandaloo —
A township where life's total sum
Is sleep, diversified with rum.

It's grass–grown streets with dust are deep,
 'Twere vain endeavour to express
The dreamless silence of its sleep,
 Its wide, expansive drunkenness.
The yearly races mostly drew
A lively crowd to Dandaloo.

There came a sportsman from the East,
 The eastern land where sportsmen blow,
And brought with him a speedy beast —
 A speedy beast as horses go.
He came afar in hope to `do'
The little town of Dandaloo.

Now this was weak of him, I wot —
 Exceeding weak, it seemed to me —
For we in Dandaloo were not
 The Jugginses we seemed to be;
In fact, we rather thought we knew
Our book by heart in Dandaloo.

We held a meeting at the bar,

And met the question fair and square —
`We've stumped the country near and far
To raise the cash for races here;
We've got a hundred pounds or two —
Not half so bad for Dandaloo.

`And now, it seems, we have to be
Cleaned out by this here Sydney bloke,
With his imported horse; and he
Will scoop the pool and leave us broke
Shall we sit still, and make no fuss
While this chap climbs all over us?'

. . . . .

The races came to Dandaloo,
And all the cornstalks from the West,
On ev'ry kind of moke and screw,
Came forth in all their glory drest.
The stranger's horse, as hard as nails,
Look'd fit to run for New South Wales.

He won the race by half a length —
QUITE half a length, it seemed to me —
But Dandaloo, with all its strength,
Roared out `Dead heat!' most fervently;
And, after hesitation meet,
The judge's verdict was `Dead heat!'

And many men there were could tell
What gave the verdict extra force:
The stewards, and the judge as well —
They all had backed the second horse.
For things like this they sometimes do
In larger towns than Dandaloo.

They ran it off; the stranger won,
Hands down, by near a hundred yards
He smiled to think his troubles done;
But Dandaloo held all the cards.
They went to scale and — cruel fate! —
His jockey turned out under–weight.

Perhaps they'd tampered with the scale!
I cannot tell. I only know
It weighed him OUT all right. I fail
To paint that Sydney sportsman's woe.
He said the stewards were a crew
Of low–lived thieves in Dandaloo.

He lifted up his voice, irate,
And swore till all the air was blue;
So then we rose to vindicate
The dignity of Dandaloo.
`Look here,' said we, `you must not poke
Such oaths at us poor country folk.'

We rode him softly on a rail,
We shied at him, in careless glee,
Some large tomatoes, rank and stale,
And eggs of great antiquity —
Their wild, unholy fragrance flew
About the town of Dandaloo.

He left the town at break of day,
He led his race–horse through the streets,
And now he tells the tale, they say,
To every racing man he meets.
And Sydney sportsmen all eschew
The atmosphere of Dandaloo.

The Geebung Polo Club

It was somewhere up the country, in a land of rock and scrub,
That they formed an institution called the Geebung Polo Club.
They were long and wiry natives from the rugged mountain side,
And the horse was never saddled that the Geebungs couldn't ride;
But their style of playing polo was irregular and rash —
They had mighty little science, but a mighty lot of dash:
And they played on mountain ponies that were muscular and strong,
Though their coats were quite unpolished,
  and their manes and tails were long.
And they used to train those ponies wheeling cattle in the scrub:
They were demons, were the members of the Geebung Polo Club.

It was somewhere down the country, in a city's smoke and steam,
That a polo club existed, called `The Cuff and Collar Team'.
As a social institution 'twas a marvellous success,
For the members were distinguished by exclusiveness and dress.
They had natty little ponies that were nice, and smooth, and sleek,
For their cultivated owners only rode 'em once a week.
So they started up the country in pursuit of sport and fame,
For they meant to show the Geebungs how they ought to play the game;
And they took their valets with them — just to give their boots a rub
Ere they started operations on the Geebung Polo Club.

Now my readers can imagine how the contest ebbed and flowed,
When the Geebung boys got going it was time to clear the road;
And the game was so terrific that ere half the time was gone

A spectator's leg was broken — just from merely looking on.
For they waddied one another till the plain was strewn with dead,
While the score was kept so even that they neither got ahead.
And the Cuff and Collar Captain, when he tumbled off to die,
Was the last surviving player — so the game was called a tie.

Then the Captain of the Geebungs raised him slowly from the ground,
Though his wounds were mostly mortal, yet he fiercely gazed around;
There was no one to oppose him — all the rest were in a trance,
So he scrambled on his pony for his last expiring chance,
For he meant to make an effort to get victory to his side;
So he struck at goal — and missed it — then he tumbled off and died.

. . . . .

By the old Campaspe River, where the breezes shake the grass,
There's a row of little gravestones that the stockmen never pass,
For they bear a crude inscription saying, `Stranger, drop a tear,
For the Cuff and Collar players and the Geebung boys lie here.'
And on misty moonlit evenings, while the dingoes howl around,
You can see their shadows flitting down that phantom polo ground;
You can hear the loud collisions as the flying players meet,
And the rattle of the mallets, and the rush of ponies' feet,
Till the terrified spectator rides like blazes to the pub —
He's been haunted by the spectres of the Geebung Polo Club.

The Travelling Post Office

The roving breezes come and go, the reed beds sweep and sway,
The sleepy river murmurs low, and loiters on its way,
It is the land of lots o' time along the Castlereagh.

. . . . .

The old man's son had left the farm, he found it dull and slow,
He drifted to the great North–west where all the rovers go.
`He's gone so long,' the old man said, `he's dropped right out of mind,
But if you'd write a line to him I'd take it very kind;
He's shearing here and fencing there, a kind of waif and stray,
He's droving now with Conroy's sheep along the Castlereagh.

`The sheep are travelling for the grass, and travelling very slow;
They may be at Mundooran now, or past the Overflow,
Or tramping down the black soil flats across by Waddiwong,
But all those little country towns would send the letter wrong,
The mailman, if he's extra tired, would pass them in his sleep,
It's safest to address the note to `Care of Conroy's sheep',
For five and twenty thousand head can scarcely go astray,
You write to `Care of Conroy's sheep along the Castlereagh'.'

. . . . .

By rock and ridge and riverside the western mail has gone,
Across the great Blue Mountain Range to take that letter on.
A moment on the topmost grade while open fire doors glare,
She pauses like a living thing to breathe the mountain air,
Then launches down the other side across the plains away
To bear that note to `Conroy's sheep along the Castlereagh'.

And now by coach and mailman's bag it goes from town to town,
And Conroy's Gap and Conroy's Creek have marked it `further down'.
Beneath a sky of deepest blue where never cloud abides,
A speck upon the waste of plain the lonely mailman rides.

Where fierce hot winds have set the pine and myall boughs asweep
He hails the shearers passing by for news of Conroy's sheep.
By big lagoons where wildfowl play and crested pigeons flock,
By camp fires where the drovers ride around their restless stock,
And past the teamster toiling down to fetch the wool away
My letter chases Conroy's sheep along the Castlereagh.

Saltbush Bill

Now this is the law of the Overland that all in the West obey,
A man must cover with travelling sheep a six–mile stage a day;
But this is the law which the drovers make, right easily understood,
They travel their stage where the grass is bad,
  but they camp where the grass is good;
They camp, and they ravage the squatter's grass till never a blade remains,
Then they drift away as the white clouds drift
  on the edge of the saltbush plains,
From camp to camp and from run to run they battle it hand to hand,
For a blade of grass and the right to pass on the track of the Overland.
For this is the law of the Great Stock Routes,
  'tis written in white and black —
The man that goes with a travelling mob must keep to a half–mile track;
And the drovers keep to a half–mile track
  on the runs where the grass is dead,
But they spread their sheep on a well–grassed run
  till they go with a two–mile spread.
So the squatters hurry the drovers on from dawn till the fall of night,

And the squatters' dogs and the drovers' dogs get mixed in a deadly fight;
Yet the squatters' men, though they hunt the mob,
  are willing the peace to keep,
For the drovers learn how to use their hands
  when they go with the travelling sheep;
But this is the tale of a Jackaroo that came from a foreign strand,
And the fight that he fought with Saltbush Bill, the King of the Overland.

Now Saltbush Bill was a drover tough, as ever the country knew,
He had fought his way on the Great Stock Routes
  from the sea to the big Barcoo;
He could tell when he came to a friendly run
  that gave him a chance to spread,
And he knew where the hungry owners were that hurried his sheep ahead;
He was drifting down in the Eighty drought
  with a mob that could scarcely creep,
(When the kangaroos by the thousands starve,
  it is rough on the travelling sheep),
And he camped one night at the crossing–place on the edge of the Wilga run,
`We must manage a feed for them here,' he said,
  `or the half of the mob are done!'
So he spread them out when they left the camp wherever they liked to go,
Till he grew aware of a Jackaroo with a station–hand in tow,
And they set to work on the straggling sheep,
  and with many a stockwhip crack
They forced them in where the grass was dead
  in the space of the half–mile track;
So William prayed that the hand of fate might suddenly strike him blue
But he'd get some grass for his starving sheep
  in the teeth of that Jackaroo.
So he turned and he cursed the Jackaroo, he cursed him alive or dead,
From the soles of his great unwieldy feet to the crown of his ugly head,
With an extra curse on the moke he rode and the cur at his heels that ran,
Till the Jackaroo from his horse got down and he went for the drover–man;
With the station–hand for his picker–up,
  though the sheep ran loose the while,

They battled it out on the saltbush plain in the regular prize–ring style.

Now, the new chum fought for his honour's sake
 and the pride of the English race,
But the drover fought for his daily bread with a smile on his bearded face;
So he shifted ground and he sparred for wind and he made it a lengthy mill,
And from time to time as his scouts came in
 they whispered to Saltbush Bill —
`We have spread the sheep with a two–mile spread,
 and the grass it is something grand,
You must stick to him, Bill, for another round
 for the pride of the Overland.'
The new chum made it a rushing fight, though never a blow got home,
Till the sun rode high in the cloudless sky
 and glared on the brick–red loam,
Till the sheep drew in to the shelter–trees and settled them down to rest,
Then the drover said he would fight no more and he gave his opponent best.

So the new chum rode to the homestead straight
 and he told them a story grand
Of the desperate fight that he fought that day
 with the King of the Overland.
And the tale went home to the Public Schools
 of the pluck of the English swell,
How the drover fought for his very life, but blood in the end must tell.
But the travelling sheep and the Wilga sheep
 were boxed on the Old Man Plain.
'Twas a full week's work ere they drafted out and hunted them off again,
With a week's good grass in their wretched hides,
 with a curse and a stockwhip crack,
They hunted them off on the road once more
 to starve on the half–mile track.
And Saltbush Bill, on the Overland, will many a time recite
How the best day's work that ever he did
 was the day that he lost the fight.

A Mountain Station

I bought a run a while ago,
On country rough and ridgy,
Where wallaroos and wombats grow —
The Upper Murrumbidgee.
The grass is rather scant, it's true,
But this a fair exchange is,
The sheep can see a lovely view
By climbing up the ranges.

And She–oak Flat's the station's name,
I'm not surprised at that, sirs:
The oaks were there before I came,
And I supplied the flat, sirs.
A man would wonder how it's done,
The stock so soon decreases —
They sometimes tumble off the run
And break themselves to pieces.

I've tried to make expenses meet,
But wasted all my labours,
The sheep the dingoes didn't eat
Were stolen by the neighbours.
They stole my pears — my native pears —
Those thrice–convicted felons,
And ravished from me unawares

My crop of paddy–melons.

And sometimes under sunny skies,
Without an explanation,
The Murrumbidgee used to rise
And overflow the station.
But this was caused (as now I know)
When summer sunshine glowing
Had melted all Kiandra's snow
And set the river going.

And in the news, perhaps you read:
`Stock passings. Puckawidgee,
Fat cattle: Seven hundred head
Swept down the Murrumbidgee;
Their destination's quite obscure,
But, somehow, there's a notion,
Unless the river falls, they're sure
To reach the Southern Ocean.'

So after that I'll give it best;
No more with Fate I'll battle.
I'll let the river take the rest,
For those were all my cattle.
And with one comprehensive curse
I close my brief narration,
And advertise it in my verse —
`For Sale! A Mountain Station.'

Been There Before

There came a stranger to Walgett town,
To Walgett town when the sun was low,
And he carried a thirst that was worth a crown,
Yet how to quench it he did not know;
But he thought he might take those yokels down,
The guileless yokels of Walgett town.

They made him a bet in a private bar,
In a private bar when the talk was high,
And they bet him some pounds no matter how far
He could pelt a stone, yet he could not shy
A stone right over the river so brown,
The Darling river at Walgett town.

He knew that the river from bank to bank
Was fifty yards, and he smiled a smile
As he trundled down, but his hopes they sank
For there wasn't a stone within fifty mile;
For the saltbush plain and the open down
Produce no quarries in Walgett town.

The yokels laughed at his hopes o'erthrown,
And he stood awhile like a man in a dream;
Then out of his pocket he fetched a stone,
And pelted it over the silent stream —
He had been there before: he had wandered down
On a previous visit to Walgett town.

The Man Who Was Away

The widow sought the lawyer's room with children three in tow,
She told the lawyer man her tale in tones of deepest woe.
Said she, `My husband took to drink for pains in his inside,
And never drew a sober breath from then until he died.

`He never drew a sober breath, he died without a will,
And I must sell the bit of land the childer's mouths to fill.
There's some is grown and gone away, but some is childer yet,
And times is very bad indeed — a livin's hard to get.

`There's Min and Sis and little Chris, they stops at home with me,
And Sal has married Greenhide Bill that breaks for Bingeree.
And Fred is drovin' Conroy's sheep along the Castlereagh,
And Charley's shearin' down the Bland, and Peter is away.'

The lawyer wrote the details down in ink of legal blue —
`There's Minnie, Susan, Christopher, they stop at home with you;
There's Sarah, Frederick, and Charles, I'll write to them to–day,
But what about the other one — the one who is away?

`You'll have to furnish his consent to sell the bit of land.'
The widow shuffled in her seat, `Oh, don't you understand?
I thought a lawyer ought to know — I don't know what to say —
You'll have to do without him, boss, for Peter is away.'

But here the little boy spoke up — said he, `We thought you knew;

He's done six months in Goulburn gaol — he's got six more to do.'
Thus in one comprehensive flash he made it clear as day,
The mystery of Peter's life — the man who was away.

The Man from Ironbark

It was the man from Ironbark who struck the Sydney town,
He wandered over street and park, he wandered up and down.
He loitered here, he loitered there, till he was like to drop,
Until at last in sheer despair he sought a barber's shop.
`'Ere! shave my beard and whiskers off, I'll be a man of mark,
I'll go and do the Sydney toff up home in Ironbark.'

The barber man was small and flash, as barbers mostly are,
He wore a strike–your–fancy sash, he smoked a huge cigar:
He was a humorist of note and keen at repartee,
He laid the odds and kept a `tote', whatever that may be,
And when he saw our friend arrive, he whispered `Here's a lark!
Just watch me catch him all alive, this man from Ironbark.'

There were some gilded youths that sat along the barber's wall,
Their eyes were dull, their heads were flat, they had no brains at all;
To them the barber passed the wink, his dexter eyelid shut,
`I'll make this bloomin' yokel think his bloomin' throat is cut.'
And as he soaped and rubbed it in he made a rude remark:
`I s'pose the flats is pretty green up there in Ironbark.'

A grunt was all reply he got; he shaved the bushman's chin,
Then made the water boiling hot and dipped the razor in.
He raised his hand, his brow grew black, he paused awhile to gloat,
Then slashed the red–hot razor–back across his victim's throat;
Upon the newly shaven skin it made a livid mark —
No doubt it fairly took him in — the man from Ironbark.

He fetched a wild up–country yell might wake the dead to hear,
And though his throat, he knew full well, was cut from ear to ear,
He struggled gamely to his feet, and faced the murd'rous foe:
`You've done for me! you dog, I'm beat! one hit before I go!
I only wish I had a knife, you blessed murdering shark!
But you'll remember all your life, the man from Ironbark.'

He lifted up his hairy paw, with one tremendous clout
He landed on the barber's jaw, and knocked the barber out.
He set to work with tooth and nail, he made the place a wreck;
He grabbed the nearest gilded youth, and tried to break his neck.
And all the while his throat he held to save his vital spark,
And `Murder! Bloody Murder!' yelled the man from Ironbark.

A peeler man who heard the din came in to see the show;
He tried to run the bushman in, but he refused to go.
And when at last the barber spoke, and said, `'Twas all in fun —
'Twas just a little harmless joke, a trifle overdone.'
`A joke!' he cried, `By George, that's fine; a lively sort of lark;
I'd like to catch that murdering swine some night in Ironbark.'

And now while round the shearing floor the list'ning shearers gape,
He tells the story o'er and o'er, and brags of his escape.
`Them barber chaps what keeps a tote, By George, I've had enough,
One tried to cut my bloomin' throat, but thank the Lord it's tough.'
And whether he's believed or no, there's one thing to remark,
That flowing beards are all the go way up in Ironbark.

The Open Steeplechase

I had ridden over hurdles up the country once or twice,
By the side of Snowy River with a horse they called `The Ace'.
And we brought him down to Sydney, and our rider Jimmy Rice,
Got a fall and broke his shoulder, so they nabbed me in a trice —
Me, that never wore the colours, for the Open Steeplechase.

`Make the running,' said the trainer, `it's your only chance whatever,
Make it hot from start to finish, for the old black horse can stay,
And just think of how they'll take it, when they hear on Snowy River
That the country boy was plucky, and the country horse was clever.
You must ride for old Monaro and the mountain boys to–day.'

`Are you ready?' said the starter, as we held the horses back,
All ablazing with impatience, with excitement all aglow;
Before us like a ribbon stretched the steeplechasing track,
And the sun–rays glistened brightly on the chestnut and the black
As the starter's words came slowly, `Are — you — ready? Go!'

Well, I scarcely knew we'd started, I was stupid–like with wonder
Till the field closed up beside me and a jump appeared ahead.
And we flew it like a hurdle, not a baulk and not a blunder,
As we charged it all together, and it fairly whistled under,
And then some were pulled behind me and a few shot out and led.

So we ran for half the distance, and I'm making no pretences
When I tell you I was feeling very nervous–like and queer,

For those jockeys rode like demons;
 you would think they'd lost their senses
If you saw them rush their horses at those rasping five foot fences —
And in place of making running I was falling to the rear.

Till a chap came racing past me on a horse they called `The Quiver',
And said he, `My country joker, are you going to give it best?
Are you frightened of the fences? does their stoutness make you shiver?
Have they come to breeding cowards by the side of Snowy River?
Are there riders on Monaro? ——' but I never heard the rest.

For I drove the Ace and sent him just as fast as he could pace it,
At the big black line of timber stretching fair across the track,
And he shot beside the Quiver. `Now,' said I, `my boy, we'll race it.
You can come with Snowy River if you're only game to face it,
Let us mend the pace a little and we'll see who cries a crack.'

So we raced away together, and we left the others standing,
And the people cheered and shouted as we settled down to ride,
And we clung beside the Quiver. At his taking off and landing
I could see his scarlet nostril and his mighty ribs expanding,
And the Ace stretched out in earnest and we held him stride for stride.

But the pace was so terrific that they soon ran out their tether —
They were rolling in their gallop, they were fairly blown and beat —
But they both were game as pebbles — neither one would show the feather.
And we rushed them at the fences, and they cleared them both together,
Nearly every time they clouted, but they somehow kept their feet.

Then the last jump rose before us, and they faced it game as ever —
We were both at spur and whipcord, fetching blood at every bound —
And above the people's cheering and the cries of `Ace' and `Quiver',
I could hear the trainer shouting, `One more run for Snowy River.'
Then we struck the jump together and came smashing to the ground.

Well, the Quiver ran to blazes, but the Ace stood still and waited,

Stood and waited like a statue while I scrambled on his back.
There was no one next or near me for the field was fairly slated,
So I cantered home a winner with my shoulder dislocated,
While the man that rode the Quiver followed limping down the track.

And he shook my hand and told me that in all his days he never
Met a man who rode more gamely, and our last set to was prime,
And we wired them on Monaro how we chanced to beat the Quiver.
And they sent us back an answer, `Good old sort from Snowy River:
Send us word each race you start in and we'll back you every time.'

The Amateur Rider

HIM going to ride for us! HIM —
  with the pants and the eyeglass and all.
Amateur! don't he just look it — it's twenty to one on a fall.
Boss must be gone off his head to be sending our steeplechase crack
Out over fences like these with an object like that on his back.

Ride! Don't tell ME he can ride.
  With his pants just as loose as balloons,
How can he sit on his horse? and his spurs like a pair of harpoons;
Ought to be under the Dog Act, he ought, and be kept off the course.
Fall! why, he'd fall off a cart, let alone off a steeplechase horse.

. . . . .

Yessir! the 'orse is all ready — I wish you'd have rode him before;
Nothing like knowing your 'orse, sir, and this chap's a terror to bore;
Battleaxe always could pull, and he rushes his fences like fun —
Stands off his jump twenty feet, and then springs like a shot from a gun.

Oh, he can jump 'em all right, sir, you make no mistake, 'e's a toff;
Clouts 'em in earnest, too, sometimes,
  you mind that he don't clout you off —
Don't seem to mind how he hits 'em, his shins is as hard as a nail,
Sometimes you'll see the fence shake
  and the splinters fly up from the rail.

All you can do is to hold him and just let him jump as he likes,
Give him his head at the fences, and hang on like death if he strikes;
Don't let him run himself out — you can lie third or fourth in the race —
Until you clear the stone wall, and from that you can put on the pace.

Fell at that wall once, he did, and it gave him a regular spread,
Ever since that time he flies it — he'll stop if you pull at his head,
Just let him race — you can trust him —
  he'll take first–class care he don't fall,
And I think that's the lot — but remember,
  HE MUST HAVE HIS HEAD AT THE WALL.

. . . . .

Well, he's down safe as far as the start,
  and he seems to sit on pretty neat,
Only his baggified breeches would ruinate anyone's seat —
They're away — here they come — the first fence,
  and he's head over heels for a crown!
Good for the new chum, he's over, and two of the others are down!

Now for the treble, my hearty — By Jove, he can ride, after all;
Whoop, that's your sort — let him fly them!
  He hasn't much fear of a fall.

Who in the world would have thought it? And aren't they just going a pace?
Little Recruit in the lead there will make it a stoutly–run race.

Lord! But they're racing in earnest — and down goes Recruit on his head,
Rolling clean over his boy — it's a miracle if he ain't dead.
Battleaxe, Battleaxe, yet! By the Lord, he's got most of 'em beat —
Ho! did you see how he struck, and the swell never moved in his seat?

Second time round, and, by Jingo! he's holding his lead of 'em well;
Hark to him clouting the timber! It don't seem to trouble the swell.
Now for the wall — let him rush it. A thirty–foot leap, I declare —
Never a shift in his seat, and he's racing for home like a hare.

What's that that's chasing him — Rataplan — regular demon to stay!
Sit down and ride for your life now!
  Oh, good, that's the style — come away!
Rataplan's certain to beat you, unless you can give him the slip;
Sit down and rub in the whalebone now — give him the spurs and the whip!

Battleaxe, Battleaxe, yet — and it's Battleaxe wins for a crown;
Look at him rushing the fences, he wants to bring t'other chap down.
Rataplan never will catch him if only he keeps on his pins;
Now! the last fence! and he's over it! Battleaxe, Battleaxe wins!

. . . . .

Well, sir, you rode him just perfect —
  I knew from the first you could ride.
Some of the chaps said you couldn't, an' I says just like this a' one side:
Mark me, I says, that's a tradesman — the saddle is where he was bred.
Weight! you're all right, sir, and thank you;
  and them was the words that I said.

On Kiley's Run

The roving breezes come and go
On Kiley's Run,
The sleepy river murmurs low,
And far away one dimly sees
Beyond the stretch of forest trees —
Beyond the foothills dusk and dun —
The ranges sleeping in the sun
On Kiley's Run.

'Tis many years since first I came
To Kiley's Run,
More years than I would care to name
Since I, a stripling, used to ride
For miles and miles at Kiley's side,
The while in stirring tones he told
The stories of the days of old
On Kiley's Run.

I see the old bush homestead now
On Kiley's Run,
Just nestled down beneath the brow
Of one small ridge above the sweep
Of river–flat, where willows weep
And jasmine flowers and roses bloom,
The air was laden with perfume
On Kiley's Run.

We lived the good old station life
On Kiley's Run,

With little thought of care or strife.
Old Kiley seldom used to roam,
He liked to make the Run his home,
The swagman never turned away
With empty hand at close of day
          From Kiley's Run.

We kept a racehorse now and then
          On Kiley's Run,
And neighb'ring stations brought their men
To meetings where the sport was free,
And dainty ladies came to see
Their champions ride; with laugh and song
The old house rang the whole night long
          On Kiley's Run.

The station hands were friends I wot
          On Kiley's Run,
A reckless, merry–hearted lot —
All splendid riders, and they knew
The `boss' was kindness through and through.
Old Kiley always stood their friend,
And so they served him to the end
          On Kiley's Run.

But droughts and losses came apace
          To Kiley's Run,
Till ruin stared him in the face;
He toiled and toiled while lived the light,
He dreamed of overdrafts at night:
At length, because he could not pay,
His bankers took the stock away
          From Kiley's Run.

Old Kiley stood and saw them go
          From Kiley's Run.

The well–bred cattle marching slow;
His stockmen, mates for many a day,
They wrung his hand and went away.
Too old to make another start,
Old Kiley died — of broken heart,
On Kiley's Run.

. . . . .

The owner lives in England now
Of Kiley's Run.
He knows a racehorse from a cow;
But that is all he knows of stock:
His chiefest care is how to dock
Expenses, and he sends from town
To cut the shearers' wages down
On Kiley's Run.

There are no neighbours anywhere
Near Kiley's Run.
The hospitable homes are bare,
The gardens gone; for no pretence
Must hinder cutting down expense:
The homestead that we held so dear
Contains a half–paid overseer
On Kiley's Run.

All life and sport and hope have died
On Kiley's Run.
No longer there the stockmen ride;
For sour–faced boundary riders creep
On mongrel horses after sheep,
Through ranges where, at racing speed,
Old Kiley used to `wheel the lead'
On Kiley's Run.

There runs a lane for thirty miles
Through Kiley's Run.
On either side the herbage smiles,
But wretched trav'lling sheep must pass
Without a drink or blade of grass
Thro' that long lane of death and shame:
The weary drovers curse the name
Of Kiley's Run.

The name itself is changed of late
Of Kiley's Run.
They call it `Chandos Park Estate'.
The lonely swagman through the dark
Must hump his swag past Chandos Park.
The name is English, don't you see,
The old name sweeter sounds to me
Of `Kiley's Run'.

I cannot guess what fate will bring
To Kiley's Run —
For chances come and changes ring —
I scarcely think 'twill always be
Locked up to suit an absentee;
And if he lets it out in farms
His tenants soon will carry arms
On Kiley's Run.

Frying Pan's Theology

Scene: On Monaro.
DRAMATIS PERSONAE:
Shock–headed blackfellow,
Boy (on a pony).
Snowflakes are falling
So gentle and slow,
Youngster says, `Frying Pan,
What makes it snow?'
Frying Pan confident
Makes the reply —
`Shake 'em big flour bag
Up in the sky!'
`What! when there's miles of it!
Sur'ly that's brag.
Who is there strong enough
Shake such a bag?'
`What parson tellin' you,
Ole Mister Dodd,
Tell you in Sunday–school?
Big feller God!
He drive His bullock dray,
Then thunder go,
He shake His flour bag —
Tumble down snow!'

The Two Devines

It was shearing–time at the Myall Lake,
 And there rose the sound thro' the livelong day
Of the constant clash that the shear–blades make
 When the fastest shearers are making play,
But there wasn't a man in the shearers' lines
That could shear a sheep with the two Devines.

They had rung the sheds of the east and west,
 Had beaten the cracks of the Walgett side,
And the Cooma shearers had giv'n them best —
 When they saw them shear, they were satisfied.
From the southern slopes to the western pines
They were noted men, were the two Devines.

'Twas a wether flock that had come to hand,
 Great struggling brutes, that the shearers shirk,
For the fleece was filled with the grass and sand,
 And seventy sheep was a big day's work.
`At a pound a hundred it's dashed hard lines
To shear such sheep,' said the two Devines.

But the shearers knew that they'd make a cheque
 When they came to deal with the station ewes;
They were bare of belly and bare of neck
 With a fleece as light as a kangaroo's.
`We will show the boss how a shear–blade shines
When we reach those ewes,' said the two Devines.

But it chanced next day when the stunted pines
 Were swayed and stirred with the dawn–wind's breath,
That a message came for the two Devines
 That their father lay at the point of death.
So away at speed through the whispering pines
Down the bridle track rode the two Devines.

It was fifty miles to their father's hut,
 And the dawn was bright when they rode away;
At the fall of night when the shed was shut
 And the men had rest from the toilsome day,
To the shed once more through the dark'ning pines
On their weary steeds came the two Devines.

`Well, you're back right sudden,' the super. said;
 `Is the old man dead and the funeral done?'
`Well, no, sir, he ain't not exactly dead,
 But as good as dead,' said the eldest son —
`And we couldn't bear such a chance to lose,
So we came straight back to tackle the ewes.'

. . . . .

They are shearing ewes at the Myall Lake,
 And the shed is merry the livelong day
With the clashing sound that the shear–blades make
 When the fastest shearers are making play,
And a couple of `hundred and ninety–nines'
Are the tallies made by the two Devines.

In the Droving Days

`Only a pound,' said the auctioneer,

`Only a pound; and I'm standing here
Selling this animal, gain or loss.
Only a pound for the drover's horse;
One of the sort that was never afraid,
One of the boys of the Old Brigade;
Thoroughly honest and game, I'll swear,
Only a little the worse for wear;
Plenty as bad to be seen in town,
Give me a bid and I'll knock him down;
Sold as he stands, and without recourse,
Give me a bid for the drover's horse.'

Loitering there in an aimless way
Somehow I noticed the poor old grey,
Weary and battered and screwed, of course,
Yet when I noticed the old grey horse,
The rough bush saddle, and single rein
Of the bridle laid on his tangled mane,
Straightway the crowd and the auctioneer
Seemed on a sudden to disappear,
Melted away in a kind of haze,
For my heart went back to the droving days.

Back to the road, and I crossed again
Over the miles of the saltbush plain —
The shining plain that is said to be
The dried–up bed of an inland sea,
Where the air so dry and so clear and bright
Refracts the sun with a wondrous light,
And out in the dim horizon makes
The deep blue gleam of the phantom lakes.

At dawn of day we would feel the breeze
That stirred the boughs of the sleeping trees,
And brought a breath of the fragrance rare
That comes and goes in that scented air;

For the trees and grass and the shrubs contain
A dry sweet scent on the saltbush plain.
For those that love it and understand,
The saltbush plain is a wonderland.
A wondrous country, where Nature's ways
Were revealed to me in the droving days.

We saw the fleet wild horses pass,
And the kangaroos through the Mitchell grass,
The emu ran with her frightened brood
All unmolested and unpursued.
But there rose a shout and a wild hubbub
When the dingo raced for his native scrub,
And he paid right dear for his stolen meals
With the drover's dogs at his wretched heels.
For we ran him down at a rattling pace,
While the packhorse joined in the stirring chase.
And a wild halloo at the kill we'd raise —
We were light of heart in the droving days.

'Twas a drover's horse, and my hand again
Made a move to close on a fancied rein.
For I felt the swing and the easy stride
Of the grand old horse that I used to ride
In drought or plenty, in good or ill,
That same old steed was my comrade still;
The old grey horse with his honest ways
Was a mate to me in the droving days.

When we kept our watch in the cold and damp,
If the cattle broke from the sleeping camp,
Over the flats and across the plain,
With my head bent down on his waving mane,
Through the boughs above and the stumps below
On the darkest night I could let him go
At a racing speed; he would choose his course,

And my life was safe with the old grey horse.
But man and horse had a favourite job,
When an outlaw broke from a station mob,
With a right good will was the stockwhip plied,
As the old horse raced at the straggler's side,
And the greenhide whip such a weal would raise,
We could use the whip in the droving days.

. . . . .

`Only a pound!' and was this the end —
Only a pound for the drover's friend.
The drover's friend that had seen his day,
And now was worthless, and cast away
With a broken knee and a broken heart
To be flogged and starved in a hawker's cart.
Well, I made a bid for a sense of shame
And the memories dear of the good old game.

`Thank you? Guinea! and cheap at that!
Against you there in the curly hat!
Only a guinea, and one more chance,
Down he goes if there's no advance,
Third, and the last time, one! two! three!'
And the old grey horse was knocked down to me.
And now he's wandering, fat and sleek,
On the lucerne flats by the Homestead Creek;
I dare not ride him for fear he'd fall,
But he does a journey to beat them all,
For though he scarcely a trot can raise,
He can take me back to the droving days.

Lost

`He ought to be home,' said the old man, `without there's something amiss.
He only went to the Two–mile — he ought to be back by this.
He WOULD ride the Reckless filly, he WOULD have his wilful way;
And, here, he's not back at sundown — and what will his mother say?

`He was always his mother's idol, since ever his father died;
And there isn't a horse on the station that he isn't game to ride.
But that Reckless mare is vicious, and if once she gets away
He hasn't got strength to hold her — and what will his mother say?'

The old man walked to the sliprail, and peered up the dark'ning track,
And looked and longed for the rider that would never more come back;
And the mother came and clutched him, with sudden, spasmodic fright:
`What has become of my Willie? — why isn't he home to–night?'

Away in the gloomy ranges, at the foot of an ironbark,
The bonnie, winsome laddie was lying stiff and stark;
For the Reckless mare had smashed him against a leaning limb,
And his comely face was battered, and his merry eyes were dim.

And the thoroughbred chestnut filly, the saddle beneath her flanks,
Was away like fire through the ranges to join the wild mob's ranks;
And a broken–hearted woman and an old man worn and grey
Were searching all night in the ranges till the sunrise brought the day.

And the mother kept feebly calling, with a hope that would not die,
`Willie! where are you, Willie?' But how can the dead reply;
And hope died out with the daylight, and the darkness brought despair,
God pity the stricken mother, and answer the widow's prayer!

Though far and wide they sought him, they found not where he fell;
For the ranges held him precious, and guarded their treasure well.
The wattle blooms above him, and the blue bells blow close by,
And the brown bees buzz the secret, and the wild birds sing reply.

But the mother pined and faded, and cried, and took no rest,
And rode each day to the ranges on her hopeless, weary quest.
Seeking her loved one ever, she faded and pined away,
But with strength of her great affection she still sought every day.

`I know that sooner or later I shall find my boy,' she said.
But she came not home one evening, and they found her lying dead,
And stamped on the poor pale features, as the spirit homeward pass'd,
Was an angel smile of gladness — she had found the boy at last.

Over the Range

Little bush maiden, wondering–eyed,
 Playing alone in the creek–bed dry,
In the small green flat on every side
 Walled in by the Moonbi ranges high;
Tell us the tale of your lonely life,
 'Mid the great grey forests that know no change.
`I never have left my home,' she said,
 `I have never been over the Moonbi Range.

`Father and mother are both long dead,
And I live with granny in yon wee place.'
`Where are your father and mother?' we said.
She puzzled awhile with thoughtful face,
Then a light came into the shy brown eye,
And she smiled, for she thought the question strange
On a thing so certain — `When people die
They go to the country over the range.'

`And what is this country like, my lass?'
`There are blossoming trees and pretty flowers,
And shining creeks where the golden grass
Is fresh and sweet from the summer showers.
They never need work, nor want, nor weep;
No troubles can come their hearts to estrange.
Some summer night I shall fall asleep,
And wake in the country over the range.'

Child, you are wise in your simple trust,
For the wisest man knows no more than you
Ashes to ashes, and dust to dust:
Our views by a range are bounded too;
But we know that God hath this gift in store,
That when we come to the final change,
We shall meet with our loved ones gone before
To the beautiful country over the range.

Only a Jockey

`Richard Bennison, a jockey, aged 14, while riding William Tell in his training, was thrown and killed. The horse is luckily uninjured.' — Melbourne Wire.

Out in the grey cheerless chill of the morning light,
 Out on the track where the night shades still lurk;
Ere the first gleam of the sungod's returning light,
 Round come the race–horses early at work.

Reefing and pulling and racing so readily,
 Close sit the jockey–boys holding them hard,
`Steady the stallion there — canter him steadily,
 Don't let him gallop so much as a yard.'

Fiercely he fights while the others run wide of him,
 Reefs at the bit that would hold him in thrall,
Plunges and bucks till the boy that's astride of him
 Goes to the ground with a terrible fall.

`Stop him there! Block him there! Drive him in carefully,
 Lead him about till he's quiet and cool.
Sound as a bell! though he's blown himself fearfully,
 Now let us pick up this poor little fool.

`Stunned? Oh, by Jove, I'm afraid it's a case with him;
 Ride for the doctor! keep bathing his head!
Send for a cart to go down to our place with him' —
 No use! One long sigh and the little chap's dead.

Only a jockey–boy, foul–mouthed and bad you see,
 Ignorant, heathenish, gone to his rest.
Parson or Presbyter, Pharisee, Sadducee,
 What did you do for him? — bad was the best.

Negroes and foreigners, all have a claim on you;
 Yearly you send your well–advertised hoard,
But the poor jockey–boy — shame on you, shame on you,
 `Feed ye, my little ones' — what said the Lord?

Him ye held less than the outer barbarian,
 Left him to die in his ignorant sin;
Have you no principles, humanitarian?
 Have you no precept — `go gather them in?'

. . . . .

Knew he God's name? In his brutal profanity,
 That name was an oath — out of many but one —
What did he get from our famed Christianity?
 Where has his soul — if he had any — gone?

Fourteen years old, and what was he taught of it?
 What did he know of God's infinite grace?
Draw the dark curtain of shame o'er the thought of it,
 Draw the shroud over the jockey–boy's face.

How M'Ginnis Went Missing

Let us cease our idle chatter,
 Let the tears bedew our cheek,
For a man from Tallangatta

Has been missing for a week.

Where the roaring flooded Murray
Covered all the lower land,
There he started in a hurry,
With a bottle in his hand.

And his fate is hid for ever,
But the public seem to think
That he slumbered by the river,
'Neath the influence of drink.

And they scarcely seem to wonder
That the river, wide and deep,
Never woke him with its thunder,
Never stirred him in his sleep.

As the crashing logs came sweeping,
And their tumult filled the air,
Then M'Ginnis murmured, sleeping,
`'Tis a wake in ould Kildare.'

So the river rose and found him
Sleeping softly by the stream,
And the cruel waters drowned him
Ere he wakened from his dream.

And the blossom–tufted wattle,
Blooming brightly on the lea,
Saw M'Ginnis and the bottle
Going drifting out to sea.

A Voice from the Town

A sequel to [Mowbray Morris's] `A Voice from the Bush'

I thought, in the days of the droving,
 Of steps I might hope to retrace,
To be done with the bush and the roving
 And settle once more in my place.
With a heart that was well nigh to breaking,
 In the long, lonely rides on the plain,
I thought of the pleasure of taking
 The hand of a lady again.

I am back into civilisation,
 Once more in the stir and the strife,
But the old joys have lost their sensation —
 The light has gone out of my life;
The men of my time they have married,
 Made fortunes or gone to the wall;
Too long from the scene I have tarried,
 And, somehow, I'm out of it all.

For I go to the balls and the races
 A lonely companionless elf,
And the ladies bestow all their graces
 On others less grey than myself;
While the talk goes around I'm a dumb one
 'Midst youngsters that chatter and prate,
And they call me `the Man who was Someone
 Way back in the year Sixty–eight.'

And I look, sour and old, at the dancers
 That swing to the strains of the band,
And the ladies all give me the Lancers,
 No waltzes — I quite understand.
For matrons intent upon matching
 Their daughters with infinite push,
Would scarce think him worthy the catching,
 The broken–down man from the bush.

New partners have come and new faces,
 And I, of the bygone brigade,
Sharply feel that oblivion my place is —
 I must lie with the rest in the shade.
And the youngsters, fresh–featured and pleasant,
 They live as we lived — fairly fast;
But I doubt if the men of the present
 Are as good as the men of the past.

Of excitement and praise they are chary,
 There is nothing much good upon earth;
Their watchword is NIL ADMIRARI,
 They are bored from the days of their birth.
Where the life that we led was a revel
 They `wince and relent and refrain' —
I could show them the road — to the devil,
 Were I only a youngster again.

I could show them the road where the stumps are
 The pleasures that end in remorse,
And the game where the Devil's three trumps are,
 The woman, the card, and the horse.
Shall the blind lead the blind — shall the sower
 Of wind reap the storm as of yore?
Though they get to their goal somewhat slower,
 They march where we hurried before.

For the world never learns — just as we did,
 They gallantly go to their fate,
Unheeded all warnings, unheeded
 The maxims of elders sedate.
As the husbandman, patiently toiling,
 Draws a harvest each year from the soil,
So the fools grow afresh for the spoiling,
 And a new crop of thieves for the spoil.

But a truce to this dull moralising,
 Let them drink while the drops are of gold,
I have tasted the dregs — 'twere surprising
 Were the new wine to me like the old;
And I weary for lack of employment
 In idleness day after day,
For the key to the door of enjoyment
 Is Youth — and I've thrown it away.

A Bunch of Roses

Roses ruddy and roses white,
 What are the joys that my heart discloses?
Sitting alone in the fading light
Memories come to me here to–night
 With the wonderful scent of the big red roses.

Memories come as the daylight fades

Down on the hearth where the firelight dozes;
Flicker and flutter the lights and shades,
And I see the face of a queen of maids
Whose memory comes with the scent of roses.

Visions arise of a scene of mirth,
And a ball–room belle that superbly poses —
A queenly woman of queenly worth,
And I am the happiest man on earth
With a single flower from a bunch of roses.

Only her memory lives to–night —
God in His wisdom her young life closes;
Over her grave may the turf be light,
Cover her coffin with roses white —
She was always fond of the big white roses.

. . . . .

Such are the visions that fade away —
Man proposes and God disposes;
Look in the glass and I see to–day
Only an old man, worn and grey,
Bending his head to a bunch of roses.

Black Swans

As I lie at rest on a patch of clover
In the Western Park when the day is done,
I watch as the wild black swans fly over
With their phalanx turned to the sinking sun;
And I hear the clang of their leader crying
To a lagging mate in the rearward flying,
And they fade away in the darkness dying,
Where the stars are mustering one by one.

Oh! ye wild black swans, 'twere a world of wonder
For a while to join in your westward flight,
With the stars above and the dim earth under,
Through the cooling air of the glorious night.
As we swept along on our pinions winging,
We should catch the chime of a church–bell ringing,
Or the distant note of a torrent singing,
Or the far–off flash of a station light.

From the northern lakes with the reeds and rushes,
Where the hills are clothed with a purple haze,
Where the bell–birds chime and the songs of thrushes
Make music sweet in the jungle maze,
They will hold their course to the westward ever,
Till they reach the banks of the old grey river,
Where the waters wash, and the reed–beds quiver
In the burning heat of the summer days.

Oh! ye strange wild birds, will ye bear a greeting
To the folk that live in that western land?
Then for every sweep of your pinions beating,
Ye shall bear a wish to the sunburnt band,
To the stalwart men who are stoutly fighting
With the heat and drought and the dust–storm smiting,
Yet whose life somehow has a strange inviting,
When once to the work they have put their hand.

Facing it yet! Oh, my friend stout–hearted,
What does it matter for rain or shine,
For the hopes deferred and the gain departed?
Nothing could conquer that heart of thine.
And thy health and strength are beyond confessing
As the only joys that are worth possessing.
May the days to come be as rich in blessing
As the days we spent in the auld lang syne.

I would fain go back to the old grey river,
To the old bush days when our hearts were light,
But, alas! those days they have fled for ever,
They are like the swans that have swept from sight.
And I know full well that the strangers' faces
Would meet us now in our dearest places;
For our day is dead and has left no traces
But the thoughts that live in my mind to–night.

There are folk long dead, and our hearts would sicken —
We would grieve for them with a bitter pain,
If the past could live and the dead could quicken,
We then might turn to that life again.
But on lonely nights we would hear them calling,
We should hear their steps on the pathways falling,
We should loathe the life with a hate appalling
In our lonely rides by the ridge and plain.

. . . . .

In the silent park is a scent of clover,
And the distant roar of the town is dead,
And I hear once more as the swans fly over
Their far–off clamour from overhead.
They are flying west, by their instinct guided,
And for man likewise is his fate decided,
And griefs apportioned and joys divided

By a mighty power with a purpose dread.

The All Right 'Un

He came from `further out',
That land of heat and drought
And dust and gravel.
He got a touch of sun,
And rested at the run
Until his cure was done,
And he could travel.

When spring had decked the plain,
He flitted off again
As flit the swallows.
And from that western land,
When many months were spanned,
A letter came to hand,
Which read as follows:

`Dear sir, I take my pen
In hopes that all your men
And you are hearty.
You think that I've forgot
Your kindness, Mr. Scott,
Oh, no, dear sir, I'm not
That sort of party.

`You sometimes bet, I know,
Well, now you'll have a show
The `books' to frighten.
Up here at Wingadee
Young Billy Fife and me
We're training Strife, and he
Is a all right 'un.

`Just now we're running byes,
But, sir, first time he tries
I'll send you word of.
And running `on the crook'
Their measures we have took,
It is the deadest hook
You ever heard of.

`So when we lets him go,
Why, then, I'll let you know,
And you can have a show
To put a mite on.
Now, sir, my leave I'll take,
Yours truly, William Blake.
P.S. — Make no mistake,
HE'S A ALL RIGHT 'UN.'

. . . . .

By next week's RIVERINE
I saw my friend had been
A bit too cunning.
I read: `The racehorse Strife
And jockey William Fife
Disqualified for life —
Suspicious running.'

But though they spoilt his game,
I reckon all the same
I fairly ought to claim
My friend a white 'un.
For though he wasn't straight,
His deeds would indicate
His heart at any rate
Was `a all right 'un'.

The Boss of the `Admiral Lynch'

Did you ever hear tell of Chili? I was readin' the other day
Of President Balmaceda and of how he was sent away.
It seems that he didn't suit 'em — they thought that they'd like a change,
So they started an insurrection and chased him across the range.
They seemed to be restless people — and, judging by what you hear,
They raise up these revolutions 'bout two or three times a year;
And the man that goes out of office, he goes for the boundary QUICK,
For there isn't no vote by ballot — it's bullets that does the trick.
And it ain't like a real battle, where the prisoners' lives are spared,
And they fight till there's one side beaten
  and then there's a truce declared,

And the man that has got the licking goes down like a blooming lord
To hand in his resignation and give up his blooming sword,
And the other man bows and takes it, and everything's all polite —
This wasn't that kind of a picnic, this wasn't that sort of a fight.

For the pris'ners they took — they shot 'em;
  no odds were they small or great,
If they'd collared old Balmaceda, they reckoned to shoot him straight.
A lot of bloodthirsty devils they were — but there ain't a doubt
They must have been real plucked 'uns — the way that they fought it out,
And the king of 'em all, I reckon, the man that could stand a pinch,
Was the boss of a one–horse gunboat. They called her the `Admiral Lynch'.

Well, he was for Balmaceda, and after the war was done,
And Balmaceda was beaten and his troops had been forced to run,
The other man fetched his army and proceeded to do things brown,
He marched 'em into the fortress and took command of the town.
Cannon and guns and horses troopin' along the road,
Rumblin' over the bridges, and never a foeman showed
Till they came in sight of the harbour, and the very first thing they see
Was this mite of a one–horse gunboat a–lying against the quay,
And there as they watched they noticed a flutter of crimson rag,
And under their eyes he hoisted old Balmaceda's flag.
Well, I tell you it fairly knocked 'em — it just took away their breath,
For he must ha' known if they caught him, 'twas nothin' but sudden death.
An' he'd got no fire in his furnace, no chance to put out to sea,
So he stood by his gun and waited with his vessel against the quay.

Well, they sent him a civil message to say that the war was done,
And most of his side were corpses, and all that were left had run;
And blood had been spilt sufficient, so they gave him a chance to decide
If he'd haul down his bit of bunting and come on the winning side.
He listened and heard their message, and answered them all polite,
That he was a Spanish hidalgo, and the men of his race MUST fight!
A gunboat against an army, and with never a chance to run,
And them with their hundred cannon and him with a single gun:
The odds were a trifle heavy — but he wasn't the sort to flinch,
So he opened fire on the army, did the boss of the `Admiral Lynch'.

They pounded his boat to pieces, they silenced his single gun,
And captured the whole consignment, for none of 'em cared to run;

And it don't say whether they shot him — it don't even give his name —
But whatever they did I'll wager that he went to his graveyard game.
I tell you those old hidalgos so stately and so polite,
They turn out the real Maginnis when it comes to an uphill fight.
There was General Alcantara, who died in the heaviest brunt,
And General Alzereca was killed in the battle's front;
But the king of 'em all, I reckon — the man that could stand a pinch —
Was the man who attacked the army with the gunboat `Admiral Lynch'.

A Bushman's Song

I'm travellin' down the Castlereagh, and I'm a station hand,
I'm handy with the ropin' pole, I'm handy with the brand,
And I can ride a rowdy colt, or swing the axe all day,
But there's no demand for a station–hand along the Castlereagh.

So it's shift, boys, shift, for there isn't the slightest doubt
That we've got to make a shift to the stations further out,
With the pack–horse runnin' after, for he follows like a dog,
We must strike across the country at the old jig–jog.

This old black horse I'm riding — if you'll notice what's his brand,
He wears the crooked R, you see — none better in the land.
He takes a lot of beatin', and the other day we tried,
For a bit of a joke, with a racing bloke, for twenty pounds a side.

It was shift, boys, shift, for there wasn't the slightest doubt

That I had to make him shift, for the money was nearly out;
But he cantered home a winner, with the other one at the flog —
He's a red–hot sort to pick up with his old jig–jog.

I asked a cove for shearin' once along the Marthaguy:
`We shear non–union here,' says he. `I call it scab,' says I.
I looked along the shearin' floor before I turned to go —
There were eight or ten dashed Chinamen a–shearin' in a row.

It was shift, boys, shift, for there wasn't the slightest doubt
It was time to make a shift with the leprosy about.
So I saddled up my horses, and I whistled to my dog,
And I left his scabby station at the old jig–jog.

I went to Illawarra, where my brother's got a farm,
He has to ask his landlord's leave before he lifts his arm;
The landlord owns the country side — man, woman, dog, and cat,
They haven't the cheek to dare to speak without they touch their hat.

It was shift, boys, shift, for there wasn't the slightest doubt
Their little landlord god and I would soon have fallen out;
Was I to touch my hat to him? — was I his bloomin' dog?
So I makes for up the country at the old jig–jog.

But it's time that I was movin', I've a mighty way to go
Till I drink artesian water from a thousand feet below;
Till I meet the overlanders with the cattle comin' down,
And I'll work a while till I make a pile, then have a spree in town.

So, it's shift, boys, shift, for there isn't the slightest doubt
We've got to make a shift to the stations further out;
The pack–horse runs behind us, for he follows like a dog,
And we cross a lot of country at the old jig–jog.

How Gilbert Died

There's never a stone at the sleeper's head,
There's never a fence beside,
And the wandering stock on the grave may tread
Unnoticed and undenied,
But the smallest child on the Watershed
Can tell you how Gilbert died.

For he rode at dusk, with his comrade Dunn
To the hut at the Stockman's Ford,
In the waning light of the sinking sun
They peered with a fierce accord.
They were outlaws both — and on each man's head
Was a thousand pounds reward.

They had taken toll of the country round,
And the troopers came behind
With a black that tracked like a human hound
In the scrub and the ranges blind:
He could run the trail where a white man's eye
No sign of a track could find.

He had hunted them out of the One Tree Hill
And over the Old Man Plain,
But they wheeled their tracks with a wild beast's skill,
And they made for the range again.
Then away to the hut where their grandsire dwelt,
They rode with a loosened rein.

And their grandsire gave them a greeting bold:
`Come in and rest in peace,
No safer place does the country hold —
With the night pursuit must cease,
And we'll drink success to the roving boys,
And to hell with the black police.'

But they went to death when they entered there,
In the hut at the Stockman's Ford,
For their grandsire's words were as false as fair —
They were doomed to the hangman's cord.
He had sold them both to the black police
For the sake of the big reward.

In the depth of night there are forms that glide
As stealthy as serpents creep,
And around the hut where the outlaws hide
They plant in the shadows deep,
And they wait till the first faint flush of dawn
Shall waken their prey from sleep.

But Gilbert wakes while the night is dark —
A restless sleeper, aye,
He has heard the sound of a sheep–dog's bark,
And his horse's warning neigh,
And he says to his mate, `There are hawks abroad,
And it's time that we went away.'

Their rifles stood at the stretcher head,
Their bridles lay to hand,
They wakened the old man out of his bed,
When they heard the sharp command:
`In the name of the Queen lay down your arms,
Now, Dunn and Gilbert, stand!'

Then Gilbert reached for his rifle true
 That close at his hand he kept,
He pointed it straight at the voice and drew,
 But never a flash outleapt,
For the water ran from the rifle breech —
 It was drenched while the outlaws slept.

Then he dropped the piece with a bitter oath,
 And he turned to his comrade Dunn:
`We are sold,' he said, `we are dead men both,
 But there may be a chance for one;
I'll stop and I'll fight with the pistol here,
 You take to your heels and run.'

So Dunn crept out on his hands and knees
 In the dim, half–dawning light,
And he made his way to a patch of trees,
 And vanished among the night,
And the trackers hunted his tracks all day,
 But they never could trace his flight.

But Gilbert walked from the open door
 In a confident style and rash;
He heard at his side the rifles roar,
 And he heard the bullets crash.
But he laughed as he lifted his pistol–hand,
 And he fired at the rifle flash.

Then out of the shadows the troopers aimed
 At his voice and the pistol sound,
With the rifle flashes the darkness flamed,
 He staggered and spun around,
And they riddled his body with rifle balls
 As it lay on the blood–soaked ground.

There's never a stone at the sleeper's head,

There's never a fence beside,
And the wandering stock on the grave may tread
Unnoticed and undenied,
But the smallest child on the Watershed
Can tell you how Gilbert died.

The Flying Gang

I served my time, in the days gone by,
In the railway's clash and clang,
And I worked my way to the end, and I
Was the head of the `Flying Gang'.
`Twas a chosen band that was kept at hand
In case of an urgent need,
Was it south or north we were started forth,
And away at our utmost speed.
If word reached town that a bridge was down,
The imperious summons rang —
`Come out with the pilot engine sharp,
And away with the flying gang.'

Then a piercing scream and a rush of steam
As the engine moved ahead,
With a measured beat by the slum and street
Of the busy town we fled,
By the uplands bright and the homesteads white,
With the rush of the western gale,

And the pilot swayed with the pace we made
 As she rocked on the ringing rail.
  And the country children clapped their hands
   As the engine's echoes rang,
  But their elders said: `There is work ahead
   When they send for the flying gang.'

Then across the miles of the saltbush plain
 That gleamed with the morning dew,
Where the grasses waved like the ripening grain
 The pilot engine flew,
A fiery rush in the open bush
 Where the grade marks seemed to fly,
And the order sped on the wires ahead,
 The pilot MUST go by.
  The Governor's special must stand aside,
   And the fast express go hang,
  Let your orders be that the line is free
   For the boys of the flying gang.

Shearing at Castlereagh

The bell is set a–ringing, and the engine gives a toot,
There's five and thirty shearers here are shearing for the loot,
So stir yourselves, you penners–up, and shove the sheep along,
The musterers are fetching them a hundred thousand strong,
And make your collie dogs speak up — what would the buyers say

In London if the wool was late this year from Castlereagh?

The man that `rung' the Tubbo shed is not the ringer here,
That stripling from the Cooma side can teach him how to shear.
They trim away the ragged locks, and rip the cutter goes,
And leaves a track of snowy fleece from brisket to the nose;
It's lovely how they peel it off with never stop nor stay,
They're racing for the ringer's place this year at Castlereagh.

The man that keeps the cutters sharp is growling in his cage,
He's always in a hurry and he's always in a rage —
`You clumsy–fisted mutton–heads, you'd turn a fellow sick,
You pass yourselves as shearers, you were born to swing a pick.
Another broken cutter here, that's two you've broke to–day,
It's awful how such crawlers come to shear at Castlereagh.'

The youngsters picking up the fleece enjoy the merry din,
They throw the classer up the fleece, he throws it to the bin;
The pressers standing by the rack are waiting for the wool,
There's room for just a couple more, the press is nearly full;
Now jump upon the lever, lads, and heave and heave away,
Another bale of golden fleece is branded `Castlereagh'.

The Wind's Message

There came a whisper down the Bland between the dawn and dark,
Above the tossing of the pines, above the river's flow;

It stirred the boughs of giant gums and stalwart ironbark;
It drifted where the wild ducks played amid the swamps below;
It brought a breath of mountain air from off the hills of pine,
A scent of eucalyptus trees in honey–laden bloom;
And drifting, drifting far away along the southern line
It caught from leaf and grass and fern a subtle strange perfume.

It reached the toiling city folk, but few there were that heard —
The rattle of their busy life had choked the whisper down;
And some but caught a fresh–blown breeze with scent of pine that stirred
A thought of blue hills far away beyond the smoky town;
And others heard the whisper pass, but could not understand
The magic of the breeze's breath that set their hearts aglow,
Nor how the roving wind could bring across the Overland
A sound of voices silent now and songs of long ago.

But some that heard the whisper clear were filled with vague unrest;
The breeze had brought its message home, they could not fixed abide;
Their fancies wandered all the day towards the blue hills' breast,
Towards the sunny slopes that lie along the riverside,
The mighty rolling western plains are very fair to see,
Where waving to the passing breeze the silver myalls stand,
But fairer are the giant hills, all rugged though they be,
From which the two great rivers rise that run along the Bland.

Oh! rocky range and rugged spur and river running clear,
That swings around the sudden bends with swirl of snow–white foam,
Though we, your sons, are far away, we sometimes seem to hear
The message that the breezes bring to call the wanderers home.
The mountain peaks are white with snow that feeds a thousand rills,
Along the river banks the maize grows tall on virgin land,
And we shall live to see once more those sunny southern hills,
And strike once more the bridle track that leads along the Bland.

Johnson's Antidote

Down along the Snakebite River, where the overlanders camp,
Where the serpents are in millions, all of the most deadly stamp;
Where the station–cook in terror, nearly every time he bakes,
Mixes up among the doughboys half–a–dozen poison–snakes:
Where the wily free–selector walks in armour–plated pants,
And defies the stings of scorpions, and the bites of bull–dog ants:
Where the adder and the viper tear each other by the throat,
There it was that William Johnson sought his snake–bite antidote.

Johnson was a free–selector, and his brain went rather queer,
For the constant sight of serpents filled him with a deadly fear;
So he tramped his free–selection, morning, afternoon, and night,
Seeking for some great specific that would cure the serpent's bite.
Till King Billy, of the Mooki, chieftain of the flour–bag head,
Told him, `Spos'n snake bite pfeller, pfeller mostly drop down dead;
Spos'n snake bite old goanna, then you watch a while you see,
Old goanna cure himself with eating little pfeller tree.'
`That's the cure,' said William Johnson, `point me out this plant sublime,'
But King Billy, feeling lazy, said he'd go another time.
Thus it came to pass that Johnson, having got the tale by rote,
Followed every stray goanna, seeking for the antidote.

. . . . .

Loafing once beside the river, while he thought his heart would break,
There he saw a big goanna fighting with a tiger–snake,
In and out they rolled and wriggled, bit each other, heart and soul,

Till the valiant old goanna swallowed his opponent whole.
Breathless, Johnson sat and watched him, saw him struggle up the bank,
Saw him nibbling at the branches of some bushes, green and rank;
Saw him, happy and contented, lick his lips, as off he crept,
While the bulging in his stomach showed where his opponent slept.
Then a cheer of exultation burst aloud from Johnson's throat;
`Luck at last,' said he, `I've struck it! 'tis the famous antidote.'

`Here it is, the Grand Elixir, greatest blessing ever known,
Twenty thousand men in India die each year of snakes alone.
Think of all the foreign nations, negro, chow, and blackamoor,
Saved from sudden expiration, by my wondrous snakebite cure.
It will bring me fame and fortune! In the happy days to be,
Men of every clime and nation will be round to gaze on me —
Scientific men in thousands, men of mark and men of note,
Rushing down the Mooki River, after Johnson's antidote.
It will cure Delirium Tremens, when the patient's eyeballs stare
At imaginary spiders, snakes which really are not there.
When he thinks he sees them wriggle, when he thinks he sees them bloat,
It will cure him just to think of Johnson's Snakebite Antidote.'

Then he rushed to the museum, found a scientific man —
`Trot me out a deadly serpent, just the deadliest you can;
I intend to let him bite me, all the risk I will endure,
Just to prove the sterling value of my wondrous snakebite cure.
Even though an adder bit me, back to life again I'd float;
Snakes are out of date, I tell you, since I've found the antidote.'

Said the scientific person, `If you really want to die,
Go ahead — but, if you're doubtful, let your sheep–dog have a try.
Get a pair of dogs and try it, let the snake give both a nip;
Give your dog the snakebite mixture, let the other fellow rip;
If he dies and yours survives him, then it proves the thing is good.
Will you fetch your dog and try it?' Johnson rather thought he would.
So he went and fetched his canine, hauled him forward by the throat.
`Stump, old man,' says he, `we'll show them we've the genwine antidote.'

Both the dogs were duly loaded with the poison–gland's contents;
Johnson gave his dog the mixture, then sat down to wait events.
`Mark,' he said, `in twenty minutes Stump'll be a–rushing round,
While the other wretched creature lies a corpse upon the ground.'
But, alas for William Johnson! ere they'd watched a half–hour's spell
Stumpy was as dead as mutton, t'other dog was live and well.
And the scientific person hurried off with utmost speed,
Tested Johnson's drug and found it was a deadly poison–weed;
Half a tumbler killed an emu, half a spoonful killed a goat,
All the snakes on earth were harmless to that awful antidote.

. . . . .

Down along the Mooki River, on the overlanders' camp,
Where the serpents are in millions, all of the most deadly stamp,
Wanders, daily, William Johnson, down among those poisonous hordes,
Shooting every stray goanna, calls them `black and yaller frauds'.
And King Billy, of the Mooki, cadging for the cast–off coat,
Somehow seems to dodge the subject of the snake–bite antidote.

Ambition and Art

Ambition

I am the maid of the lustrous eyes

Of great fruition,
Whom the sons of men that are over–wise
Have called Ambition.

And the world's success is the only goal
I have within me;
The meanest man with the smallest soul
May woo and win me.

For the lust of power and the pride of place
To all I proffer.
Wilt thou take thy part in the crowded race
For what I offer?

The choice is thine, and the world is wide —
Thy path is lonely.
I may not lead and I may not guide —
I urge thee only.

I am just a whip and a spur that smites
To fierce endeavour.
In the restless days and the sleepless nights
I urge thee ever.

Thou shalt wake from sleep with a startled cry,
In fright upleaping
At a rival's step as it passes by
Whilst thou art sleeping.

Honour and truth shall be overthrown
In fierce desire;
Thou shalt use thy friend as a stepping–stone
To mount thee higher.

When the curtain falls on the sordid strife
That seemed so splendid,

Thou shalt look with pain on the wasted life
 That thou hast ended.

Thou hast sold thy life for a guerdon small
 In fitful flashes;
There has been reward — but the end of all
 Is dust and ashes.

For the night has come and it brings to naught
 Thy projects cherished,
And thine epitaph shall in brass be wrought —
 `He lived and perished.'

Art

I wait for thee at the outer gate,
 My love, mine only;
Wherefore tarriest thou so late
 While I am lonely.

Thou shalt seek my side with a footstep swift,
 In thee implanted
Is the love of Art and the greatest gift
 That God has granted.

And the world's concerns with its rights and wrongs
 Shall seem but small things —
Poet or painter, a singer of songs,
 Thine art is all things.

For the wine of life is a woman's love
 To keep beside thee;
But the love of Art is a thing above —
 A star to guide thee.

As the years go by with thy love of Art
All undiminished,
Thou shalt end thy days with a quiet heart —
Thy work is finished.

So the painter fashions a picture strong
That fadeth never,
And the singer singeth a wond'rous song
That lives for ever.

The Daylight is Dying

The daylight is dying
Away in the west,
The wild birds are flying
In silence to rest;
In leafage and frondage
Where shadows are deep,
They pass to its bondage —
The kingdom of sleep.
And watched in their sleeping
By stars in the height,
They rest in your keeping,
Oh, wonderful night.

When night doth her glories

Of starshine unfold,
'Tis then that the stories
Of bush–land are told.
Unnumbered I hold them
In memories bright,
But who could unfold them,
Or read them aright?
Beyond all denials
The stars in their glories
The breeze in the myalls
Are part of these stories.
The waving of grasses,
The song of the river
That sings as it passes
For ever and ever,
The hobble–chains' rattle,
The calling of birds,
The lowing of cattle
Must blend with the words.
Without these, indeed, you
Would find it ere long,
As though I should read you
The words of a song
That lamely would linger
When lacking the rune,
The voice of the singer,
The lilt of the tune.

But, as one half–hearing
An old–time refrain,
With memory clearing,
Recalls it again,
These tales, roughly wrought of
The bush and its ways,
May call back a thought of
The wandering days,

And, blending with each
 In the mem'ries that throng,
There haply shall reach
 You some echo of song.

In Defence of the Bush

So you're back from up the country, Mister Townsman, where you went,
And you're cursing all the business in a bitter discontent;
Well, we grieve to disappoint you, and it makes us sad to hear
That it wasn't cool and shady — and there wasn't plenty beer,
And the loony bullock snorted when you first came into view;
Well, you know it's not so often that he sees a swell like you;
And the roads were hot and dusty, and the plains were burnt and brown,
And no doubt you're better suited drinking lemon–squash in town.
Yet, perchance, if you should journey down the very track you went
In a month or two at furthest you would wonder what it meant,
Where the sunbaked earth was gasping like a creature in its pain
You would find the grasses waving like a field of summer grain,
And the miles of thirsty gutters blocked with sand and choked with mud,
You would find them mighty rivers with a turbid, sweeping flood;
For the rain and drought and sunshine make no changes in the street,
In the sullen line of buildings and the ceaseless tramp of feet;
But the bush hath moods and changes, as the seasons rise and fall,
And the men who know the bush–land — they are loyal through it all.

. . . . .

But you found the bush was dismal and a land of no delight,
Did you chance to hear a chorus in the shearers' huts at night?
Did they `rise up, William Riley' by the camp–fire's cheery blaze?
Did they rise him as we rose him in the good old droving days?
And the women of the homesteads and the men you chanced to meet —
Were their faces sour and saddened like the `faces in the street',
And the `shy selector children' — were they better now or worse
Than the little city urchins who would greet you with a curse?
Is not such a life much better than the squalid street and square
Where the fallen women flaunt it in the fierce electric glare,
Where the sempstress plies her sewing till her eyes are sore and red
In a filthy, dirty attic toiling on for daily bread?
Did you hear no sweeter voices in the music of the bush
Than the roar of trams and 'buses, and the war–whoop of `the push'?
Did the magpies rouse your slumbers with their carol sweet and strange?
Did you hear the silver chiming of the bell–birds on the range?
But, perchance, the wild birds' music by your senses was despised,
For you say you'll stay in townships till the bush is civilised.
Would you make it a tea–garden and on Sundays have a band
Where the `blokes' might take their `donahs',
 with a `public' close at hand?
You had better stick to Sydney and make merry with the `push',
For the bush will never suit you, and you'll never suit the bush.

Last Week

Oh, the new–chum went to the back block run,
But he should have gone there last week.
He tramped ten miles with a loaded gun,
But of turkey or duck he saw never a one,
For he should have been there last week,
 They said,
There were flocks of 'em there last week.

He wended his way to a waterfall,
And he should have gone there last week.
He carried a camera, legs and all,
But the day was hot, and the stream was small,
For he should have gone there last week,
 They said.
They drowned a man there last week.

He went for a drive, and he made a start,
Which should have been made last week,
For the old horse died of a broken heart;
So he footed it home and he dragged the cart —
But the horse was all right last week,
 They said.
He trotted a match last week.

So he asked the bushies who came from far
To visit the town last week,
If they'd dine with him, and they said `Hurrah!'
But there wasn't a drop in the whisky jar —
You should have been here last week,
 He said,
I drank it all up last week!

Those Names

The shearers sat in the firelight, hearty and hale and strong,
After the hard day's shearing, passing the joke along:
The `ringer' that shore a hundred, as they never were shorn before,
And the novice who, toiling bravely, had tommy–hawked half a score,
The tarboy, the cook, and the slushy, the sweeper that swept the board,
The picker–up, and the penner, with the rest of the shearing horde.
There were men from the inland stations
  where the skies like a furnace glow,
And men from the Snowy River, the land of the frozen snow;
There were swarthy Queensland drovers who reckoned all land by miles,
And farmers' sons from the Murray, where many a vineyard smiles.
They started at telling stories when they wearied of cards and games,
And to give these stories a flavour they threw in some local names,
And a man from the bleak Monaro, away on the tableland,
He fixed his eyes on the ceiling, and he started to play his hand.

He told them of Adjintoothbong, where the pine–clad mountains freeze,
And the weight of the snow in summer breaks branches off the trees,
And, as he warmed to the business, he let them have it strong —
Nimitybelle, Conargo, Wheeo, Bongongolong;
He lingered over them fondly, because they recalled to mind
A thought of the old bush homestead, and the girl that he left behind.
Then the shearers all sat silent till a man in the corner rose;
Said he, `I've travelled a–plenty but never heard names like those.
Out in the western districts, out on the Castlereagh
Most of the names are easy — short for a man to say.

`You've heard of Mungrybambone and the Gundabluey pine,
Quobbotha, Girilambone, and Terramungamine,

Quambone, Eunonyhareenyha, Wee Waa, and Buntijo —'
But the rest of the shearers stopped him:
`For the sake of your jaw, go slow,
If you reckon those names are short ones out where such names prevail,
Just try and remember some long ones before you begin the tale.'
And the man from the western district, though never a word he said,
Just winked with his dexter eyelid, and then he retired to bed.

A Bush Christening

On the outer Barcoo where the churches are few,
And men of religion are scanty,
On a road never cross'd 'cept by folk that are lost,
One Michael Magee had a shanty.

Now this Mike was the dad of a ten year old lad,
Plump, healthy, and stoutly conditioned;
He was strong as the best, but poor Mike had no rest
For the youngster had never been christened.

And his wife used to cry, `If the darlin' should die
Saint Peter would not recognise him.'
But by luck he survived till a preacher arrived,
Who agreed straightaway to baptise him.

Now the artful young rogue, while they held their collogue,
With his ear to the keyhole was listenin',

And he muttered in fright, while his features turned white,
`What the divil and all is this christenin'?'

He was none of your dolts, he had seen them brand colts,
And it seemed to his small understanding,
If the man in the frock made him one of the flock,
It must mean something very like branding.

So away with a rush he set off for the bush,
While the tears in his eyelids they glistened —
`'Tis outrageous,' says he, `to brand youngsters like me,
I'll be dashed if I'll stop to be christened!'

Like a young native dog he ran into a log,
And his father with language uncivil,
Never heeding the `praste' cried aloud in his haste,
`Come out and be christened, you divil!'

But he lay there as snug as a bug in a rug,
And his parents in vain might reprove him,
Till his reverence spoke (he was fond of a joke)
`I've a notion,' says he, `that'll move him.'

`Poke a stick up the log, give the spalpeen a prog;
Poke him aisy — don't hurt him or maim him,
'Tis not long that he'll stand, I've the water at hand,
As he rushes out this end I'll name him.

`Here he comes, and for shame! ye've forgotten the name —
Is it Patsy or Michael or Dinnis?'
Here the youngster ran out, and the priest gave a shout —
`Take your chance, anyhow, wid `Maginnis'!'

As the howling young cub ran away to the scrub
Where he knew that pursuit would be risky,
The priest, as he fled, flung a flask at his head

That was labelled `MAGINNIS'S WHISKY'!

And Maginnis Magee has been made a J.P.,
And the one thing he hates more than sin is
To be asked by the folk, who have heard of the joke,
How he came to be christened `Maginnis'!

How the Favourite Beat Us

`Aye,' said the boozer, `I tell you it's true, sir,
I once was a punter with plenty of pelf,
But gone is my glory, I'll tell you the story
How I stiffened my horse and got stiffened myself.

`'Twas a mare called the Cracker, I came down to back her,
But found she was favourite all of a rush,
The folk just did pour on to lay six to four on,
And several bookies were killed in the crush.

`It seems old Tomato was stiff, though a starter;
They reckoned him fit for the Caulfield to keep.
The Bloke and the Donah were scratched by their owner,
He only was offered three–fourths of the sweep.

`We knew Salamander was slow as a gander,
The mare could have beat him the length of the straight,
And old Manumission was out of condition,

And most of the others were running off weight.

`No doubt someone `blew it', for everyone knew it,
The bets were all gone, and I muttered in spite
`If I can't get a copper, by Jingo, I'll stop her,
Let the public fall in, it will serve the brutes right.'

`I said to the jockey, `Now, listen, my cocky,
You watch as you're cantering down by the stand,
I'll wait where that toff is and give you the office,
You're only to win if I lift up my hand.'

`I then tried to back her — `What price is the Cracker?'
`Our books are all full, sir,' each bookie did swear;
My mind, then, I made up, my fortune I played up
I bet every shilling against my own mare.

`I strolled to the gateway, the mare in the straightway
Was shifting and dancing, and pawing the ground,
The boy saw me enter and wheeled for his canter,
When a darned great mosquito came buzzing around.

`They breed 'em at Hexham, it's risky to vex 'em,
They suck a man dry at a sitting, no doubt,
But just as the mare passed, he fluttered my hair past,
I lifted my hand, and I flattened him out.

`I was stunned when they started, the mare simply darted
Away to the front when the flag was let fall,
For none there could match her, and none tried to catch her —
She finished a furlong in front of them all.

`You bet that I went for the boy, whom I sent for
The moment he weighed and came out of the stand —
`Who paid you to win it? Come, own up this minute.'
`Lord love yer,' said he, `why you lifted your hand.'

\`'Twas true, by St. Peter, that cursed \`muskeeter'
Had broke me so broke that I hadn't a brown,
And you'll find the best course is when dealing with horses
To win when you're able, and KEEP YOUR HANDS DOWN.

The Great Calamity

MacFierce'un came to Whiskeyhurst
 When summer days were hot,
And bided there wi' Jock McThirst,
 A brawny brother Scot.
Gude Faith! They made the whisky fly,
 Like Highland chieftains true,
And when they'd drunk the beaker dry
 They sang \`We are nae fou!'

 \`There is nae folk like oor ain folk,
  Sae gallant and sae true.'
 They sang the only Scottish joke
  Which is, \`We are nae fou.'

Said bold McThirst, \`Let Saxons jaw
 Aboot their great concerns,
But bonny Scotland beats them a',
 The land o' cakes and Burns,
The land o' partridge, deer, and grouse,

Fill up your glass, I beg,
There's muckle whusky i' the house,
Forbye what's in the keg.'

And here a hearty laugh he laughed,
`Just come wi' me, I beg.'
MacFierce'un saw with pleasure daft
A fifty–gallon keg.

`Losh, man, that's grand,' MacFierce'un cried,
`Saw ever man the like,
Now, wi' the daylight, I maun ride
To meet a Southron tyke,
But I'll be back ere summer's gone,
So bide for me, I beg,
We'll make a grand assault upon
Yon deevil of a keg.'

. . . . .

MacFierce'un rode to Whiskeyhurst,
When summer days were gone,
And there he met with Jock McThirst
Was greetin' all alone.
`McThirst what gars ye look sae blank?
Have all yer wits gane daft?
Has that accursed Southron bank
Called up your overdraft?
Is all your grass burnt up wi' drouth?
Is wool and hides gone flat?'
McThirst replied, `Gude friend, in truth,
'Tis muckle waur than that.'

`Has sair misfortune cursed your life
That you should weep sae free?
Is harm upon your bonny wife,

The children at your knee?
Is scaith upon your house and hame?'
McThirst upraised his head:
`My bairns hae done the deed of shame —
'Twere better they were dead.

`To think my bonny infant son
Should do the deed o' guilt —
HE LET THE WHUSKEY SPIGOT RUN,
AND A' THE WHUSKEY'S SPILT!'

. . . . .

Upon them both these words did bring
A solemn silence deep,
Gude faith, it is a fearsome thing
To see two strong men weep.

Come-by-Chance

As I pondered very weary o'er a volume long and dreary —
For the plot was void of interest — 'twas the Postal Guide, in fact,
There I learnt the true location, distance, size, and population
Of each township, town, and village in the radius of the Act.

And I learnt that Puckawidgee stands beside the Murrumbidgee,
And that Booleroi and Bumble get their letters twice a year,

Also that the post inspector, when he visited Collector,
Closed the office up instanter, and re–opened Dungalear.

But my languid mood forsook me, when I found a name that took me,
Quite by chance I came across it — `Come–by–Chance' was what I read;
No location was assigned it, not a thing to help one find it,
Just an N which stood for northward, and the rest was all unsaid.

I shall leave my home, and forthward wander stoutly to the northward
Till I come by chance across it, and I'll straightway settle down,
For there can't be any hurry, nor the slightest cause for worry
Where the telegraph don't reach you nor the railways run to town.

And one's letters and exchanges come by chance across the ranges,
Where a wiry young Australian leads a pack–horse once a week,
And the good news grows by keeping, and you're spared the pain of weeping
Over bad news when the mailman drops the letters in the creek.

But I fear, and more's the pity, that there's really no such city,
For there's not a man can find it of the shrewdest folk I know,
`Come–by–chance', be sure it never means a land of fierce endeavour,
It is just the careless country where the dreamers only go.

. . . . .

Though we work and toil and hustle in our life of haste and bustle,
All that makes our life worth living comes unstriven for and free;
Man may weary and importune, but the fickle goddess Fortune
Deals him out his pain or pleasure, careless what his worth may be.

All the happy times entrancing, days of sport and nights of dancing,
Moonlit rides and stolen kisses, pouting lips and loving glance:
When you think of these be certain you have looked behind the curtain,
You have had the luck to linger just a while in `Come–by–chance'.

Under the Shadow of Kiley's Hill

This is the place where they all were bred;
 Some of the rafters are standing still;
Now they are scattered and lost and dead,
Every one from the old nest fled,
 Out of the shadow of Kiley's Hill.

Better it is that they ne'er came back —
 Changes and chances are quickly rung;
Now the old homestead is gone to rack,
Green is the grass on the well–worn track
 Down by the gate where the roses clung.

Gone is the garden they kept with care;
 Left to decay at its own sweet will,
Fruit trees and flower beds eaten bare,
Cattle and sheep where the roses were,
 Under the shadow of Kiley's Hill.

Where are the children that throve and grew
 In the old homestead in days gone by?
One is away on the far Barcoo
Watching his cattle the long year through,
 Watching them starve in the droughts and die.

One in the town where all cares are rife,
 Weary with troubles that cramp and kill,

Fain would be done with the restless strife,
Fain would go back to the old bush life,
 Back to the shadow of Kiley's Hill.

One is away on the roving quest,
 Seeking his share of the golden spoil,
Out in the wastes of the trackless west,
Wandering ever he gives the best
 Of his years and strength to the hopeless toil.

What of the parents? That unkept mound
 Shows where they slumber united still;
Rough is their grave, but they sleep as sound
Out on the range as on holy ground,
 Under the shadow of Kiley's Hill.

Jim Carew

Born of a thoroughbred English race,
 Well proportioned and closely knit,
Neat of figure and handsome face,
 Always ready and always fit,
Hard and wiry of limb and thew,
That was the ne'er–do–well Jim Carew.

One of the sons of the good old land —
 Many a year since his like was known;

Never a game but he took command,
 Never a sport but he held his own;
Gained at his college a triple blue —
Good as they make them was Jim Carew.

Came to grief — was it card or horse?
 Nobody asked and nobody cared;
Ship him away to the bush of course,
 Ne'er–do–well fellows are easily spared;
Only of women a tolerable few
Sorrowed at parting with Jim Carew.

Gentleman Jim on the cattle camp,
 Sitting his horse with an easy grace;
But the reckless living has left its stamp
 In the deep drawn lines of that handsome face,
And a harder look in those eyes of blue:
Prompt at a quarrel is Jim Carew.

Billy the Lasher was out for gore —
 Twelve–stone navvy with chest of hair,
When he opened out with a hungry roar
 On a ten–stone man it was hardly fair;
But his wife was wise if his face she knew
By the time you were done with him, Jim Carew.

Gentleman Jim in the stockmen's hut
 Works with them, toils with them, side by side;
As to his past — well, his lips are shut.
 `Gentleman once,' say his mates with pride;
And the wildest Cornstalk can ne'er outdo
In feats of recklessness, Jim Carew.

What should he live for? A dull despair!
 Drink is his master and drags him down,
Water of Lethe that drowns all care.

Gentleman Jim has a lot to drown,
And he reigns as king with a drunken crew,
Sinking to misery, Jim Carew.

Such is the end of the ne'er–do–well —
Jimmy the Boozer, all down at heel;
But he straightens up when he's asked to tell
His name and race, and a flash of steel
Still lightens up in those eyes of blue —
`I am, or — no, I WAS — Jim Carew.'

The Swagman's Rest

We buried old Bob where the bloodwoods wave
At the foot of the Eaglehawk;
We fashioned a cross on the old man's grave,
For fear that his ghost might walk;
We carved his name on a bloodwood tree,
With the date of his sad decease,
And in place of `Died from effects of spree',
We wrote `May he rest in peace'.

For Bob was known on the Overland,
A regular old bush wag,
Tramping along in the dust and sand,
Humping his well–worn swag.
He would camp for days in the river–bed,

And loiter and `fish for whales'.
`I'm into the swagman's yard,' he said,
`And I never shall find the rails.'

But he found the rails on that summer night
For a better place — or worse,
As we watched by turns in the flickering light
With an old black gin for nurse.
The breeze came in with the scent of pine,
The river sounded clear,
When a change came on, and we saw the sign
That told us the end was near.

But he spoke in a cultured voice and low —
`I fancy they've "sent the route";
I once was an army man, you know,
Though now I'm a drunken brute;
But bury me out where the bloodwoods wave,
And if ever you're fairly stuck,
Just take and shovel me out of the grave
And, maybe, I'll bring you luck.

`For I've always heard —' here his voice fell weak,
His strength was well-nigh sped,
He gasped and struggled and tried to speak,
Then fell in a moment — dead.
Thus ended a wasted life and hard,
Of energies misapplied —
Old Bob was out of the `swagman's yard'
And over the Great Divide.

. . . . .

The drought came down on the field and flock,
And never a raindrop fell,
Though the tortured moans of the starving stock

Might soften a fiend from hell.
And we thought of the hint that the swagman gave
When he went to the Great Unseen —
We shovelled the skeleton out of the grave
To see what his hint might mean.

We dug where the cross and the grave posts were,
We shovelled away the mould,
When sudden a vein of quartz lay bare
All gleaming with yellow gold.
'Twas a reef with never a fault nor baulk
That ran from the range's crest,
And the richest mine on the Eaglehawk
Is known as `The Swagman's Rest'.

Printed in the United States
71061LV00004B/34

9 781419 171468